THE SOUND OF THE SUBURBS

999

JILTED JOHN

by JILTED JOHN

DESTINATION VENUS

REZILLOS

pretty vacant

Sex Pistols

GOD Save THE QUEEN

Sex Pistols

Siouxsie and the Banshees

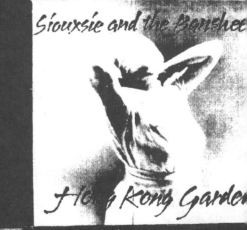

Hong Kong Garden

SPIZZENERGI

No More Heroes

SQUEEZE

COOL FOR KATS

'SOMETHING BETTER CHANG
STRAIGHTEN OUT

Making Plans for Nigel

PUNK!

AN A–Z

BARRY LAZELL

Bounty
Books

PUNK!

Editor: Mike Evans
Assistant Editor: Humaira Husain
Production Controller: Melanie Franz
Picture Research: Liz Fowler
Design: Valerie Hawthorn and Steve Byrne
Thanks to: Ben Barrett and Louise Leffler

First published in 1995 by Hamlyn,
a division of Octopus Publishing Group Ltd

This edition published 2005 by Bounty Books,
a division of Octopus Publishing Group Ltd
2–4 Heron Quays, London E14 4JP

ISBN 0 7537 1221 0
ISBN13 9780753712214

A CIP catalogue record for this book is available
from the British Library

Printed and bound in China

AN A - Z

PUNK!

FOREWORD

A PHARMACUTICAL HISTORY OF G MINOR

It was only in the years following the appearance of The Sex Pistols that I came to realise how valuable the pharmacology and energy of the Punk Rock movement, which spawned derivative examples elsewhere around the globe, was to Music in general. It had far reaching results. Not least was in the way and manner that music in a small community grew and expanded. Tom Verlaine of Television had left the UK with vivid memories of salivasoaked clothes and slam-dancing zealots. This was, of course, part of the natural Punk landscape. In an equally improbable way, the spearhead of the punk fashion and music had as its icon and hate figure – Her Majesty the Queen. Pinks and blacks were the team colors, and slashing designs were the graffiti modes that

came to predominate. Fashion and music again rained on everyone, as in the days of Swinging London and Carnaby Street. The stages of fashion, from Mary Quant to Vivienne Westwood, are determinates of a whole stylistic apparition – the dramatic send-up of the unglamorous English outside the gentry, forced to labour in windowless rapture. They are all characters on a string.

This book details the dramatis personae of the period. It also shows, equally interestingly, the incidental, internecine wanderings of the many musicians who travelled from one incarnation to the other, mixing and re-mixing their musical styles in the following years. This is not to say that those movements elsewhere were any less genuine in their thrust and ambitions, nor that they found less fertile social or political soil where they flourished. The French had their day ,as did the Angelenos. It was, however, obvious that in the UK there was a political attitude surrounding the most ecstatic of these manifestations; and the fact that the most aggressive milieu for it in America was found in LA was reinforced by a social dynamic in which the distance between rich and poor was most marked. These were very captive audiences, no matter what the size.

In August 1975, when I returned to London from New York and the Patti Smith Album, I looked forward to being reunited with The Spedding Band and a European Tour which was fuelled liberally by the violence of these leather-chain & safety-pin audiences. A year later after moving back to New York and working with a local group, I again returned with them to London to pick up where I left off. I was handed my head on a platter. It was another reminder of the sharp differences between NY and London rock styles. That band seemed frozen in another time... No leather. No chains. No hairglue. No chance.

The stage had grown crowded.

Who all the various characters were, where they came from and went to in this period is to be found in this book. Although the categories are here to be read about, it is the texture of those individual efforts of shared hostility, in an imaginary tapestry littered with philistine obstacles that is, in the end, absorbing.

We are all the better for it and this telling of it by Barry Lazell.

John Cale

INTRODUCTION

The punk era is a fascinating part of the overall history of rock music, because it represents one of those occasional, and seemingly inevitable, pauses to kick over the traces. By the mid-1970s, the musical revolution instituted by the Beatles – which had amounted to a cultural conquering of the world – was more than a decade old. The thrusting young growth sprouted so many roots and branches that they seemed to have precious little room to manoeuvre any more. In the early 1970s the main stem was, basically, progressive rock, grown vastly corporate, self-indulgent, and expensive to create, produce, package and perform. It also required a degree of musical virtuosity, which generally lay in the hands of musicians who had come along in the 60s in the Beatles' wake, and who had genuinely progressed to great proficiency and status. Such musicians were, by definition, old (ie, they weren't teenagers, and most would not be seeing the poorer side of 30 again): the new, young intake of boys and girls fired by the same spirt as John Lennon or Mick Jagger 10 years earlier were effectively disenfranchised by the state of rock as it stood.

And so, punk. Young musicians, inspired by the do-it-yourself-and-upset-the-bastards attitude of a few pioneers, turned their collective back on where rock had progressed to, and took it again from basics, freely borrowing from the noisiest, angriest, most fired-up spots of genius they were able to spot in what had gone before – often acts who had already tested the mainstream at an earlier time, but been swatted aside by it. Many of the new generation were similarly swatted; punk did not conquer the world commercially – however, many people whom that 70s punk spark first wound up and placed on the track, did move on to international and lasting success. Some of them, 20 years after it all started, are important pillars of the rock world of the 90s. Some day, at a time and in a manner which nobody can predict, a new bunch of snotty kids with the chip of musical disenfranchisement on their shoulders, will kick over this lot's traces too.

This book makes no extravagant claims to be the definitive, considered history of punk as a musican and sociological phenomenon. That book, I would suggest, has already been written – by Jon Savage in *England's Dreaming* – and if you haven't read that, you owe it to your musical education to nip down to the library and borrow a copy. (I'm not daft - I want you to actually buy *this* book.) What we have attempted between these covers are the individual histories of the many acts who were instrumental in creating, building, attaching themselves to, or in some cases sprouting out of, the punk movement of the mid-1970s to the early 1980s. The full list of everyone with some sort of valid claim to inclusion here runs to hundreds, and inevitably we have had to be selective. Sometimes the choice of who to keep in and who to exclude was a tough one, notably with regard to the many acts who fall, in some way, on the blurred defining line between punk and other musical styles. Some of our ommissions may irritate you, as may some of our inclusions: my editor and myself learned very quickly that everybody's jugements in these matters are different. We happen to think we have included here reference to everyone who actually mattered in punk: if you disagree, don't complain to us, but go and play a record by the artist we've left out. Then, someday, you or someone may include them in a book, too. If punk wasn't about the fleetingness of the fabled fifteen minutes of fame, then what was?

Barry Lazell

"ANARCHY IN THE U.K"

A sex

BANNED IN THE U.K

.....JELLO BIAFRA/VOGALS.....L.E. RAY/GUITARS.....

.KLAUS FLUORIDE/BASS,VOCALS.....BRUCE SLESINGER/

.....PRODUCED BY GEZA X & DI

NEW WA

℗ & © 1980

RECORDS,

GARDENS SQUARE, LONDON

PINNACLE

ADAM AND THE ANTS

The group which would become the UK's biggest teen pop sensation of 1980-81 had its roots in a lower-key and less commercially-motivated late-70s punk band of the same name. The original Adam & The Ants came together in April 1977, from the remnants of the B-Sides, a group formed in mid-1976 at Hornsey School Of Art in North London. Vocalist Adam Ant (real name Stuart Goddard, a veteran of still earlier Hornsey School Of Art pub-circuit band Bazooka Joe), guitarist Lester Square (who must also have had a real name) and bassist Andy Warren all carried over from the earlier outfit, which had rehearsed and put some songs together, but failed

to find any live work. The newcomer was drummer Paul Flanagan. Square departed almost immediately after their first gig, at London's Roxy Club, and would later resurface in the Monochrome Set. His place was taken by Mark Gaumont, who powered the band through a series of London gigs which brought them to the attention of Jordan, Malcolm McLaren's would-be-media-star assistant at his Sex shop.

By the Autumn of 1977, both Gaumont and Flanagan had flown the nest, making way for Dave Barbe on drums and Johnny Bivouac on guitar. However, via the Jordan connection (she became the Ants' manager and

Adam Ant with Jordan

also part-time vocalist), the band came to the attention of Malcolm McLaren and The Pistols camp in general, joining in the controversial Jubilee Day Thames boat trip, and getting signed up to play musical cameos alongside Jordan in Derek Jarman's punk movie *Jubilee*. They cut versions of their two most fully rounded songs, 'Deutscher Girls' and 'Plastic Surgery', for both the film and its soundtrack album, but otherwise failed to attract any notable record company interest. So, with a bondage gear image which was clearly McLaren-influenced, they concentrated on live club gigs around London, headlining the launch of punk club The Vortex alongside the also still-unsigned Siouxsie & The Banshees.

1978 saw their first nationwide tour gigs, but a split with Jordan, who went off to pursue her acting ambitions. A potentially more serious loss was that of Bivouac, who curiously left to join his predecessor Mark Gaumont's band, but Matthew Ashman, formerly of the Kameras, proved to be a solid replacement, and it was as a quartet (Ant, Warren, Ashman and Barbe) that they eventually signed a recording deal with Decca towards the end of the year. A single, 'Young Parisians', was issued to little interest, but the band's live reputation was now strong enough to win them both a European tour and their first UK trek as headliners, as well as some John Peel BBC radio sessions. The Decca deal quickly soured, partly because the once-mighty label was now in terminal crisis. An album was almost fully recorded but not issued (Decca would later attempt unsuccessfully to release it as a cash-in during Adam's early superstar years), and the group left, to sign instead to the new independent Do It label. Here, the first single, 'Zerox', also flopped initially, but would prove to be a steady indie chart hit during the following year. However, following the recording of the 'Do It' album 'Dirk Wears White Sox', Andy Warren moved on to join his old cohort Lester Square in the Monochrome Set, and the band got yet another new member in the person of Leigh Gorman.

They also acquired a new svengali, in the shape of Malcolm McLaren (his involvement with The Pistols well behind him), whom Adam asked in, on a £1000 consultancy fee, in order to mastermind their push to a wider audience. He was presumably more than a little taken aback by McLaren's response, which was to back the other three Ants when they unilaterally pushed Adam from the band, citing dissatisfaction with their role as side men. Vocalist and band split at the end of January 1980, after which McLaren immediately paired the others with teenage girl vocalist Annabella L'Win as Bow Wow Wow, while Adam was left with the Ants' name, to

form a new band from scratch. The outfit he put together with his guitarist friend Marco Pirroni would, within 18 months and with a totally re-invented image and musical style, become the hottest act in the country, and one of the biggest record sellers of the 80s, although their musical connections to the punk scene were effectively severed from 1980 onwards. However, Adam's early punk material would come back to haunt him: during 1981 a reissued 'Young Parisians' would make the top 10 alongside his current hits, and as late as 1982, the even earlier and more primitive 'Deutscher Girls' from Jubilee would reach No.13 on opportunistic reissue.

Recommended CD listening: 'Dirk Wears White Sox' (Columbia Rewind 480521-2)

THE ADICTS

East Anglia's leading punk outfit of the early 80s, The Adicts, from Ipswich, overcame some initial confusion with another indie band named The Addix by a very strong, if controversial, visual image, which, with its combination of face paint and black bowlers, clearly drew its inspiration from Stanley Kubrick's banned movie of futuristic thug culture, A Clockwork Orange.

The quartet comprised vocalist Keith Warren, otherwise known as Monkey, guitarist Pete Davidson, bassist Mel Ellis and drummer Kid Dee (actually Michael Davison) Too late on the scene to have any direct link with the initial wave of UK punk bands, they went all-out to push a hard, traditionally anarchistic style at the time when the commercial scene was yielding to synthesisers and the New Romantics, and possibly because of their strong, if stylised, stage image, they managed a commercial purple patch — at least in terms of the indie charts — as they label-hopped between the likes of Dining Out (which released their first vinyl outing, the tongue-in-cheek EP 'Lunch With The Adicts'), DWED, Razor and Fall Out. They had strong-selling albums with 'Songs Of Praise' and 'Sound Of Music' (the MOR-like titles having become a speciality), and were scoring major indie chart hits with angry-sounding singles like 'Chinese Takeaway' and 'Bad Boy' as late as 1983. In fact, the band seems never to have gone away, and would resurface semi-regularly on the indie scene fringes in the late 80s and early 90s with occasional albums (including a couple of live sets) aimed at the younger generation punk nostalgia circuit.

Recommended CD listening: 'The Complete Adicts Singles Collection' (Anagram CDPUNK 33)

The Adicts

The Adverts, with Gaye second left

THE ADVERTS

Formed early in 1976 in London, The Adverts, comprising T.V. Smith on vocals, Howard Pickup on guitar, Laurie Driver on drums, and panda-eyed female bassist (and obvious visual focus) Gaye Advert, were one of the first bands to become a familiar fixture at the Roxy club in Covent Garden, and made their vinyl debut performing the lifestyle-celebrating 'Bored Teenagers' on Harvest's live compilation album from the venue. In a fairly short space of time they had toured alongside The Damned at Brian James' invitation, and via that connection cut a single for Stiff, to which The Damned were also signed. 'One-Chord Wonders' was widely interpreted as being tongue-in-cheek self-deprecatory, but in fact was a tight, energetic thrash that, for all its comparative lack of sales at the time, is retrospectively regarded as one of the greatest early UK punk singles.

The Stiff release, along with the rock media interest in Gaye's visual appeal, prompted the much larger Anchor Records to snap up the band early in 1977, and their next single, 'Gary Gilmore's Eyes' (a reference to a recent American executee), was driven by a catchy, commercial chorus line into the UK Top 20. Peaking at No.18, it was one of the earliest punk singles to find significant commercial sales. It also, however, marked the peak of The Adverts' fame: by the time their album 'Crossing The Red Sea With The Adverts' was released at the start of 1978, there was critical acclaim, but only enough concentrated sales to give the set a one-week stay in the chart. (Ironically, this has also come, in recent years, to be

regarded as one of the classic punk milestones, with original copies of the release commanding high collector prices in the 1990s).

One further peer-group-identifying single 'No Time To Be 21', also made a chart showing, after which the bubble had burst, and a move to the even bigger RCA Records did nothing to reinflate it, with the album 'Cast Of Thousands' plummeting to instant oblivion. During 1978, Driver was replaced on drums by, in fairly quick succession, John Towe (from Generation X) and Rod Latter, and during 1979 Pickup and Advert also split the ranks. Left to shoulder the band's career on his own, Smith wound things up by leading a new line-up through some final college dates in October 1979, and then promptly disbanding the outfit. He re-emerged during the early 80s in lower-key fashion at the head of T.V. Smith's Explorers, but never managed to recapture The Adverts' archetypal fifteen glorious minutes of punk fame.

Recommended CD listening: 'Crossing The Red Sea With The Adverts' (Link CLINK 001CD)

ALTERNATIVE TV

Mark Perry, who was one of the seminal figures of the New Wave as the editor of *Sniffin' Glue*, the first and most famous punk fanzine (see later entry), was inevitably quickly drawn himself into the burgeoning punk band scene as both a writer and performer. In March 1977, Perry put together Alternative TV (more normally referred to as 'ATV'), a quartet that comprised himself as vocalist, Scotsman Alex Fergusson on guitar, Tyrone Thomas on bass, and John Towe, a former short-time member of Chelsea and Generation X, on drums. Towe left early on to form The Rage, and was replaced in the drum seat by Chris Bennett; thereafter interminable changes of personnel proved to one of ATV's hallmarks, so much so that they often played as just a trio.

Unstable or not, the band were prolific enough on vinyl, after launching themselves via 'Love Lies Limp', a flexi-single given away with copies of *Sniffin' Glue*. Their label, Deptford Fun City, its ironic name taken from the high-rise London borough where Mark P produced the early issues of his fanzine, became one of the first wave of punk-orientated indies, and went on to release four ATV albums (one shared with Here And Now, another a live tape of an early gig at the Rat Club) within two years, plus a batch of singles that included 'Action Time Vision', 'Life After Life', 'You Bastard' and 'The Force Is Blind'.

None of ATV's releases, however, sold particularly well, and by March of 1979, Mark Perry, disillusioned by what he saw as the major labels' hijacking and subsequent commercialisation of the punk scene, had had enough of live gigging as well, and officially disbanded the group. Despite this he set up a new outfit, The Good Missionaries, almost immediately, which also cut an album for Deptford Fun City, but would eventually return with a more 80s-orientated (and recording only) ATV, again with no great commercial success. Guitarist Alex Fergusson, meanwhile, went on to enjoy a slightly higher profile in Psychic TV.

Recommended CD listening: 'The Image Has Cracked (The A.T.V. Punk Collection') (Anagram CDPUNK 24)

ANAGRAM RECORDS

Although it was not even in existence during the original punk era of the late 1970s, the London-based Anagram label has, in latter times, played a vibrant and vital role in keeping a wide swathe of classic punk repertoire available on the market. Launched in 1982 as a subsidiary to the already long-serving UK indie Cherry Red, initially as a home for 'bands that we published that didn't really fit on the Cherry Red label', as founder Iain McNay later put it, Anagram soon found its own niche in the indie field. Commercial success came with acts like Alien Sex Fiend, The Vibrators and Vice Squad, and also with a series of anthologies of early punk singles under the banner Punk And Disorderly. From this latter initiative evolved a policy, begun in the second half of the 80s and continuing into the present, of acquiring the rights to the repertoires of (mostly) punk-oriented bands which had ceased to be, and of independent labels which had ceased trading. Aided fortuitously by the huge growth market in back-catalogue purchase on CD, this programme has led to the still ongoing creation of a catalogue offering a wide panorama of British punk music from both its first 1970s flush and the 80s 'second wave'. Notably, there are CD anthologies devoted exclusively to the key output of labels like Good Vibrations, No Future, Raw, Secret, Riot City and others – including Anagram itself. Moreover, most punk acts with significant repertoires now have definitive Anagram compilations of their own – The Angelic Upstarts, Discharge, The

Adicts, Eater, The Notsensibles and The Suburban Studs are among the many repackaged for posterity. Anagram Records' played a major role in keeping the less stellar names of punk available and in the public ear during the 1990s, and this contribution cannot be overrated.

Recommended CD listening: 'Anagram Records: The Punk Singles Collection' (Anagram CDPUNK 37)

THE ANGELIC UPSTARTS

The first flowering of punk from North-East England, the deceptively cutely named Angelic Upstarts formed in mid-1977 in South Shields. Original members Mensi (vocals), Mond (guitar), Steve (bass) and Decca (drums) were all from the Brockley Whims Housing Estate, and were inspired to articulate their local version of the teenage wasteland after hearing The Sex Pistols and The Clash. With their near-monosyllabic names and ultra tough appearance, plus Memsi's savagely abrasive vocals and a distinct anti-establishment stance on most of their early material, the band developed a (probably) deliberately unnerving hard man image which would later be imitated widely by many of the second generation of anarchistic inclined punk bands, circa 1981.

In contrast to the apparent National Front leanings of some of the later 'hard cases', however, The Upstarts' political motivations revolved strongly around social justice, as evidenced by their debut single 'The Murder Of Liddle Towers', prompted by an alleged incident of police brutality. Released in the summer of 78, it was at first self-financed and distributed, before being picked up by indie distributor Small Wonder, which gave the track national exposure. Talk of a deal with Polydor ensued, though this was allegedly scuppered by fisticuffs between Mensi and a Polydor employee, and the band was signed instead to Warner Bros. at the beginning of 1979 – with bassist Ronnie Wooden in place of Steve, who had been evicted because of drug problems.

The Upstarts scored five UK hit singles in 12 months on Warner, though only the second, 'Teenage Warning', (barely) cracked the Top 30, and its follow-ups peaked progressively lower. Two Warner albums, 'Teenage Warning' and 'We Gotta Get Out Of This Place', made Nos. 29 and 54 respectively. In search of better results, the band moved across to EMI's Zonophone label in mid-1980, but although they had two further hit singles and two more chart albums via that outlet in 1981, the momentum had clearly slowed considerably by now – the album 'Still From The Heart', in 1982, failed to chart at all. The band were a popular live act from the start, their gigs nonetheless tended to attract violence, partly a response to the band's tough image, but also increasingly due to right-wing elements opposed to their socialist stance. This eventually took its toll on the Upstarts' commercial appeal, as did their material, with its hardcore punk ethos, which was less amenable to stylistic change than that of, for instance, their original idols The Clash. Although staying intact until 1986, they were commercially marginalised some time earlier. Reformations have occurred since, most recently in 1992, when Roadrunner Records released an album titled 'Bombed Out', but the still untamed Mensi's energies these days are mostly directed to anti-fascist politics rather than music.

Recommended CD listening: 'Angel Dust'(The Collected Highs 1978-83) (Anagram CDMGRAM 7)

ANTI-NOWHERE LEAGUE

The Anti-Nowhere League were late arrivals on – in fact, something of a coda to – the original UK punk movement, since they were not formed (in straight laced Tunbridge Wells ironically) until the second half of 1980, by which time most of the constituents of the original scene had disappeared or mutated well beyond punk's basics. Nevertheless, they summed up the archetypal punk stance of 1976, from a name which was all-encompassing negativity, to music which largely preached the same nihilistic outlook, couched in raw, loud anger or sarcastic humour. Initially making their name in London via gigs at the Lyceum, they came to rapid national attention on the Apocalypse Punk Tour in 1981, playing alongside The Exploited, Discharge, Anti Pasti and Chron Gen.

Comprising Animal (vocals), Magoo (guitar), Winston (bass) and P.J. (drums), the band's near-monosyllabic professional names, echoing the grunted monikers of The Angelic Upstarts and others, also spoke volumes about the way they wished to be perceived. As for their own perceptions of the rest of the world, their December 1981 debut single (for the indie WXYZ label, run by punk promoter John Curd) was a curiously-chosen update of folkie Ralph McTell's hit 'Streets Of London', which earned the distinction – after selling several thousand and topping the indie chart – of an Obscene Publications Squad seizure of all remaining copies from the distributor's warehouse, on the grounds that the B-side, 'So What', featured obscene lyrics. The band called their subsequent headlining trek around the UK the So What Tour, and the title of their follow-up 'I Hate People/Let's Break The Law' was possibly justified, as well as being predictable. 1982 saw two further strong – selling singles in 'Woman' and 'For You', and also an album - 'We Are The League' – which sold well enough to make the national top 30, despite songs ironically vilifying or contemptuous of virtually everything in sight.

By 1985, following a period of reduced recording activity (and by which time Jonathan Birch had replaced P.J. on drums), The League showed strong signs of edging towards the rock mainstream on the album 'The Perfect Crime', cut for heavy rock label GWR, but neither their old punk fans or any new ones particularly wanted to know about the more polished sound on offer, and meagre sales became the catalyst of the band going their separate ways, following a notably triumphal farewell gig on their home Tunbridge Wells turf. The early 1990s, however, would see the band re-grouping in their original style to tour on the back of the new wave of nostalgia for early punk.

Recommended CD listening: 'Complete Singles Collection' (Anagram Punk Collectors Series CD PUNK 44)

The Anti-Nowhere League's Animal is attacked on stage by Rat Scabies

ANTI-PASTI

Derbyshire's chief contribution to British punk, Anti-Pasti were a quartet comprising Martin Roper (vocals), Dugi (guitar), Stu (bass) and Stan (drums), who came together at the tail-end of 1979 at the time when basic punk was beginning to undergo a revival. They were signed a few months later by the indie label Rondolet, based in nearby Mansfield, becoming only the second act on the label (the first being heavy metal band Witchfynde. Solid gig popularity, especially around their native midlands, helped propel their first release, an EP titled 'Four Sore Points', containing four socially-conscious rants. into the indie charts. Almost immediately, there was a change of personnel in the rhythm section, with new bassists and drummer Kev and Will (Anti-Pasti never believed in names of more than one syllable) arriving in time for the three-track follow-up single 'Let Them Free' – another indie chart success.

1981 was the band's best year. They toured with Discharge, The Exploited, Chron Gen and The Anti-Nowhere League on the highly popular Apocalypse Punk national one-nighter trek, and their debut album 'The Last Call' was not only a success in the indie market, but crossed over for some weeks to the national LP chart, where it peaked just below the Top 30. The next single, 'Six Guns', actually topped the indie chart, while 'Don't Let Them Grind You Down', a one-off collaboration with The Exploited for the Superville label, went one better still, showing up (albeit only at No.70) in the national UK singles chart.

1982 saw a recording hiatus and the addition of a second guitarist to the gigging line-up, in the shape of Olly Hoon, but the next single 'East To The West', and the second album 'Caution In The Wind' sold disappointing by the standards of previous successes. Not being ones to stand around analysing a drop-off in popularity, Anti-Pasti did the punk thing and split up at the end of the year, sensibly in good time before their core audience had chance to get bored with them.

Recommended CD listening: 'The Last Call 'Anagram Punk Collectors Series' CD PUNK 48)

Opposite page, Anti-Nowhere's Animal

B

BIG IN JAPAN

Though never really big anywhere, this aggregation were something of a minor legend in their native Merseyside area, and were also an early home to several individuals who went on to be very big indeed elsewhere. First formed in May 1977 in Liverpool, the band was initially a trio of Clash fans comprising Bill Drummond (vocals and guitar), Kevin Ward (vocals and bass) and Phil Allen (drums). After just a handful of gigs, they also drafted in additional guitarist Ian Broudie and vocalist Jayne Casey, while Clive Langer (who fronted the seminal Deaf School before becoming a highly successful producer) also played with them a few times – including on their first single. This was an odd affair on which they shared a side apiece with an outfit called The Chuddy Nuddies (in reality, The Yachts). The first release on the Eric's label (launched by the local club of the same name), the single was billed on its sleeve as being 'Brutality - Religion and a Dance Beat', and the Big In Japan side featured them on a song also titled 'Big In Japan', in which the title was virtually the only audible lyric.

No sooner was the single in the shops, in November '77, than original members Ward and Allen left, to be replaced by Holly Johnson (who arrived just in time for their first London gig on November 28) on bass, and Budgie (previously with Julian Cope and Pete Wylie in the short-lived Nova Mob) on drums. This was to be Big In Japan's most stable line-up, and gigged widely around the country for more than six months, with a visually powerful, theatrically-slanted set. When, come the Summer of 1978, they were beginning to attract record company interest (principally from Jet and Stiff), Johnson departed to go solo, and David Balfe (ex-Dalek I Love You) joined as bass player. His tenure was to be shorter-lived, however, since immediately after passing an audition gig for Stiff, the band paradoxically decided to split, bowing out with an appropriate farewell appearance at Eric's at the end of August.

Bill Drummond started up his own Merseyside indie label, Zoo Records, and launched it with a posthumous Big In Japan EP, 'From Y To Z And Never Again', rounding up the four of the few additional recordings the band had made during its existence. Drummond and Balfe would also regroup as Lori and The Chameleons before Balfe joined The Teardrop Explodes. Arguably the biggest success for both men, though, would come a decade or so later, when Drummond would be half of the chartbusting KLF, and Balfe would launch Food Records, home of Blur. Later stardom was also to accrue to Holly Johnson (lead singer with Frankie Goes To Hollywood), Budgie (drummer with Siouxsie & The Banshees) and Ian Broudie (under the group pseudonym The Lightning Seeds), and to a lesser extent to Jayne Casey (vocalist with Pink Military).

THE BIRTHDAY PARTY

Australia's major contribution to the early international punk scene came together in Melbourne while still at school, and began gigging as The Boys Next Door upon leaving school in 1977, with a line-up of Nick Cave (vocals), Mick Harvey (guitar), Tracy Pew (bass) and Phil Calvert (drums). A second guitarist, Roland Howard, joined late in 1978, and the band cut an album, 'Door Door', for the established Melbourne label Mushroom, early the following year. Relations between label and band were poor, however, this being mostly due to the latter's refusal to move on commercially from their uncompromisingly raw and alienated musical stance.

The band decided upon a new start, cut an indie EP titled 'Hee Haw', and shifted their base during 1980 from Australia to Britain, where they were signed by the fledgling 4AD label, an offshoot of Beggars Banquet.

Birthday Party (above) and Black Flag (far right)

Radio 1 DJ John Peel quickly became a champion, and their initial 4AD single 'The Friend Catcher' and their album 'Prayers On Fire' (the latter recorded back home in Australia) were well received critically in the UK, both releases also reaching the indie chart.

1981 saw their biggest UK indie hit, the gothic-styled 'Release The Bats', and also a collaboration with American punkette Lydia Lunch, who supported them on a UK tour. Their vinyl effort together was the one-side-apiece 12" single 'Drunk On The Pope's Blood/The Agony Is The Ecstasy'.

In 1982, back in Britain after an Australian tour (and temporarily minus Tracy Pew, languishing for a while in an Oz jail after a drink-driving charge), the band cut a new album, 'Junkyard', which actually made the UK national chart (albeit only at No.73), indicating no let-up in their strong fan support. However, the members themselves were experiencing musical itchy feet, and decamped to Berlin before the end of the year, in order to develop new work out of the British media spotlight. Drummer Calvert was asked to leave at the same time, and he would move on to join The Psychedelic Furs. The four-piece band continued on into 1983, although without apparently gaining much in the way of musical inspiration from their Berlin exile, and it became apparent that the remaining players had different, separate, musical agendas. They played a final Spring 1983 tour of Australia, and fittingly wound up The Birthday Party with a farewell gig in their home town Melbourne in June. Howard and Harvey would shortly

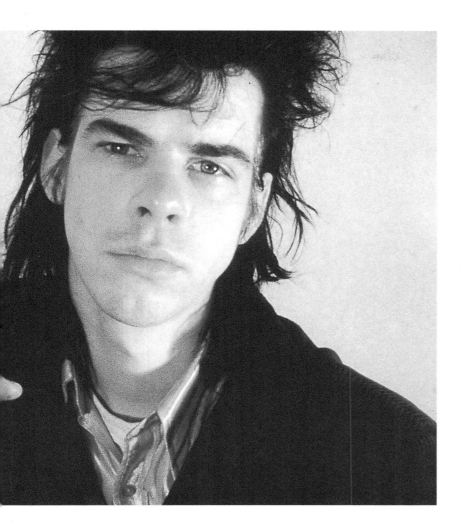

be up and running again in Crime And The City Solution, while Nick Cave began a fruitful solo career which would encompass recording, acting, novel writing, and, in the mid-1980s, the formation of another successful outfit, The Bad Seeds.

Recommended CD listening: Prayers On Fire (4AD CAD 104 CD)

BLACK FLAG

Formed late in 1976 by guitarist Greg Ginn and vocalist Keith Morris, Black Flag were one of Los Angeles' very first bands to espouse the angry, anti-establishment essence of punk, at a time when most of the West Coast was still awash with Eagles clones and virtuoso session man albums. Adding Charles Dukowski on bass and Brian Migdol on drums, they played club gigs for over a year before launching their own indie label, SST Records, in 1978 with their four-track EP 'Nervous Breakdown''.Towards the end of 1979, Morris left to form his own band, The Circle Jerks, and he was eventually replaced in July 1980 as lead vocalist by Henry Rollins, formerly of hardcore band SOA (State Of Alert). In fact, the line-up suffered several upheavals around this time, before they settled down as Ginn, Rollins, Dukowski, Dez Cadena on guitar and Puerto Rican drummer Robo by the time of the mid-1981 sessions for the band's first album 'Damaged'. A deal was reached by the major MCA label for the LP's release, but this was annulled after MCA's bosses actually

heard the proposed record: one was quoted as saying 'As a parent, I find it an anti-parent record.' Nevertheless, the album did finally appear, towards the end of the year, on a joint Unicorn/SST label, with the printed MCA logo on the sleeve stickered over. It had a completely independent distribution, and went on to sell well.

From here on, Black Flag as a live act and SST as an alternative recording outlet were pretty well inseparable, with Dukowski dropping out of the band to take an administrative role, and develop a roster which also drew in the likes of Husker Du, Sonic Youth and Dinosaur Jr. Further albums by Black Flag included 'Everything Went Black', 'My War', and 'Family Man' – the latter showcasing Rollins' non-singing alter ego as an aggressive spoken-word poet and orator.

Frequently subject to personnel changes between albums, the band eventually outlived its usefulness as a unit to both Ginn and Rollins, and officially broke up in 1986. SST continued with Ginn nurturing several like-minded bands and his own projects, while Rollins formed The Henry Rollins Band and found international – if not mainstream – success with his uncompromising music, prose (his talent widened to include books) and poetry. His reputation in the 1990s is as one of rock music's foremost – perhaps *the* foremost – spoken word artist, while his music has lost nothing of the uncompromising aggression associated with Black Flag.

Recommended CD listening: 'The First Four Years' (SST SSTCD 002)

Punk!

Debbie Harry and Blondie

BLITZ

This quartet, with a visual image encompassing both skinhead cuts and braces and longish hair and massed tattoos, were arguably Manchester's leading contribution to the resurgent early 1980s UK punk scene under the Oi! banner. The first act signed to the new No Future label, towards the end of 1981, they also provided its first release in December with the EP 'All Out Attack', a compilation of four 'smash the system' – type songs which sold out its first pressing (1000 copies) within days and shot straight into the indie chart – a feat emulated by a strong of follow-up singles like 'Never Surrender', 'Warriors' and the EP 'Total Noise', which their anthem 'Voice Of A Generation' shared with tracks by similarly-inclined acts The Business, The Gonads and Dead Generation. They also played alongside some of these compatriots on the earnestly-motivated (but long-windedly dubbed) Oi! Against Racism And Political Extremism But Still Against The System punk package tour of the UK.

Blitz's major commercial achievement, which put them among the absolute elite of the Oi! movement, was to score a national Top 30 album in the UK. Released in October 1982, their debut LP 'Voice Of A Generation' not only held the No.2 slot on the indie chart for several weeks, but also had a three-week run in the mainstream listings, where it peaked at No.27. A later set on Future Records, 'Second Empire Justice', was rather more moderately successful.

Recommended CD listening: 'The Complete Blitz Singles Collection' (Anagram CDPUNK 25)

BLONDIE

Although they would become the archetypal commercial new wave pop band during their years of fame, Blondie's origins were deeply entrenched in the mid-1970s New York punk scene. The band evolved from the Stilettos, a trio of 60s-orientated girl singers (Debbie Harry, Elda Gentile and Rosie Ross) backed by an instrumental trio led by Chris Stein. They lasted from mid-1973 until August 1974, when they regrouped as Angel & The Snakes, with Debbie as solo vocalist. By early 1975, this band had become Blondie & The Banzai Babes, and they were gigging regularly in New York City at CBGB's and The Performance Studio, performing songs such as 'In The Flesh', 'Platinum Blonde', and the Shangri-Las' oldie 'Out In The Streets'.

1975 saw a lot of personnel comings and goings, until finally in February 1976 the band solidified in a five-piece line-up comprising Harry (vocals), Stein (guitar), Jimmy Destri (keyboards), Gary Valentine (bass) and Clem Burke (drums), and with a name finally shortened to Blondie (somewhat to Harry's chagrin, as she had wanted to stop peroxiding her hair, but now felt obliged to continue). The former New York Dolls manager Marty Thau had them record a single, coupling 'X Offender' and 'In The Sun', for a new label he was planning, but was so pleased with the results that he offered the disc to Private Stock Records, which in turn offered a deal to cut the debut album 'Blondie', on which Blondie worked with the veteran New York producer Richard Gottehrer.

Both the album and a new single, 'In The Flesh' appeared early in 1977, at which time Blondie also undertook their first US tour and visited the UK, where they played alongside fellow Americans Talking Heads and garnered plenty of rock press coverage. They also attracted the attention of Chrysalis Records, which bought out their Private Stock contract, reissued the first album, and set the band on what would be a fairly rapid ride to international stardom – beginning in the UK, where the second album 'Plastic Letters' and the single 'Denis' would be major hits early in 1978. By then, most practical and stylistic ties to the punk scene were effectively severed – as were those with Gary Valentine, who was replaced on bass by Frank Infante in July 1977. The remainder of the story is a familiar part of mainstream rock history.

Recommended CD listening: 'Blondie' (Chrysalis VK 41165) and 'The Best Of Blondie' (Chrysalis CCD 1371)

Bob Geldof (left) with The Boomtown Rats

BOOMTOWN RATS

The Boomtown Rats were formed in Dun Laoghaire, near Dublin in the Irish Republic, during the latter half of 1975. Bob Geldof (vocals), Garry Roberts (guitar), Gerry Cott (guitar), Johnny Fingers (keyboards), Pete Briquette (bass) and Simon Crowe (drums) were mostly former students, bent on making music to avoid having to take daytime jobs, and they actually settled on their name on the night of their first public gig at a Dublin high school in November 1975 – Geldof found it in a book he was reading about the American folk singer Woody Guthrie.

Several months of Irish gigging later, the band found themselves pursued by five UK labels, and settled on a deal with Phonogram, via its Ensign subsidiary. A UK tour followed during the first half of 1977, including some dates with US visitors Tom Petty & The Heartbreakers. The Rats' first single, 'Looking After No.1', shot to No.11 on the chart, and launched a series of similar high-energy, anthemic singles ('Mary Of The Fourth Form', 'Like Clockwork') which would culminate in the No.1 successes 'Rat Trap' and 'I Don't Like Mondays' in 1978 and 1979.

Although the band initially appealed to the same punk audiences as The Sex Pistols and The Clash, and their live gigs were raucous affairs in front of wildly pogoing crowds, Geldof was an erudite writer and performer whose musical and lyrical concerns were already transcending those of the nihilistic 1977 punk ethos by the time of The Boomtown Rats' first hits. Both their 1977 debut album 'The Boomtown Rats' and its 1978 follow-up 'A Tonic For The Troops' amply demonstrated this, and were sufficiently strong that the lost allegiance of any punks was made up many times by a wider commercial following. It seems likely that Geldof, happy to ride punk's coat-tails into the spotlight, anticipated making such an early exit from the genre from the beginning.

The Rats followed a successful commercial career through the early 1980s, but were sublimated to Geldof's charity concerns from the time of Band Aid at Christmas 1984 – although the band did have a prestigious slot on the July 1985 Live Aid concert at Wembley. Geldof, however, was to opt for a (moderately successful) solo recording career in the later 80s.

THE BOYS

The Boys, purveyors of a revved-up (and sometimes tongue-in-cheek) brand of power-pop which dovetailed them neatly into the early punk scene, were formed in London in June 1976 after guitarist Matt Dangerfield and Norwegian keyboard player Casino Steel (formerly of the Hollywood Brats) had flirted briefly with the never-quite-fully-formed London SS. This duo, after starting to write material together, linked up with 'Honest' John Plain (guitar), who was already putting together the basis of a band with Duncan 'Kid' Reid (vocals and bass) and Jack Black (drums). They signed to NEMS Records early in 1977, releasing a single, 'I Don't Care', in

and 'Boys Only', however the band would consistently fail to translate their proven on-stage appeal into further record success. Steel was the first to leave, and after a final, nothing-doing single for the Parole label in October 1981, they split up.

A peculiar footnote to The Boys' story is their alter-ego incarnation as The Yobs, which occurred only at Christmas time! In December 1977, '78 and '79, they released tongue-in-cheek Christmas singles under the Yobs' name, including a bizarre version of 'Silent Night' to rival that by The Dickies, and a cover of Chuck Berry's 'Run Rudolph Run' with a sleeve that pictured former Nazi boss Rudolf Hess running as directed. The joke came to a head in 1979, when Safari released an entire 'Yobs Christmas Album' of similar mock-rock material.

THE BROMLEY CONTINGENT

This key group of people, though not performers as such, were arguably Britain's first punk fans. The original core of the Bromley Contingent were in the audience of one of the first Sex Pistols gigs, at Ravensbourne Art College in Bromley, an outer London suburb on the border with Kent. In stark contrast to the apathetic or appalled reaction of most early Pistols audiences

April, and their debut album 'The Boys' in July. The latter was their only UK chart success, reaching a modest No.50, but both the single and its follow-up 'The First Time' charted in various Benelux and Scandinavian countries, and the band became a solid on-stage attraction on the new wave circuit both in Britain and on the continent, providing tour support for ex-Velvet and punk guru John Cale in Spring 1977.

Towards the end of 1979, the band shifted to the independent Safari Records, where Dangerfield was also occupied in production work for the label's recent signing Toyah. Several more singles were released over the next two years, along with a couple of albums, 'To Hell With The Boys'

(including the bulk of the one at Ravensbourne), this group began to both spread infectious word-of-mouth praise around their acquaintances, and become a regular fixture at all the band's gigs in and around the capital – attracting notice from the music press as they started dressing for audience participation in outrageous and provocative home-made fashions which rapidly became identified with the spread of punk itself.

Principal Contingent members were Simon Barker, who first alerted his friends to The Pistols' unique appeal after witnessing that first Bromley gig, Sue Ballion (who was to become Siouxsie), Steve Severin (later a Banshee), Billy Broad (quickly to metamorphose into Billy Idol), John Beverley (a future

Above and top, the Bromley Contingent
Opposite, The Buzzcocks

Pistol himself, as Sid Vicious) and the striking Catwoman (Sue Lucas). Most of these would be seen on TV on the occasion of the Bill Grundy/Sex Pistols contretemps, and they were very much the prototypes for the general media perception of what constituted a punk fan in the mid-late 1970s.

THE BUSINESS

This South London quartet, formed during 1979, became a leading part of the early 1980s Oi! revival of British punk, which stomped simplicity, aggression and working-class disenfranchisement back into the music after two years of new wave diversification. They played on a package tour billed as Oi! Against Racism And Political Extremism But Still Against The System, which helped identify their personal politics, if only anybody could be bothered to decipher its rather unwieldy wordiness. The band's earliest incarnation lasted until just before Christmas 1981, surviving the Southall riot in July that year which followed The 4-Skins' ill-fated gig at the Hamborough Tavern (they were the support act), but breaking up soon after Secret Records released their first single, 'Harry May'. The label kept their name alive with a version of 'Step Into Christmas' on its various-artists punk Yuletide EP 'Bollocks To Christmas', and was rewarded six months later when The Business reformed in a slightly amended line-up, and delivered a highly-rated single, 'Smash The Discos.'

Then, in what was either an oddly-judged scam or a freakish bit of thievery, the tapes for what was proposed as their first album, 'Loud, Proud And Punk' went permanently missing, forcing the band to re-record most of the material, which eventually appeared, with some very positive critical reaction, at the end of 1982 as 'Suburban Rebels'.

After Secret closed down in 1983, the band moved on through other

labels like Syndicate, Wonderful World Of and Diamond, tempering their style with more pop/rock sensibility, and remained active as a live unit until almost the end of the decade, when they finally split.

Recommended CD listening: 3 tracks on 'The Secret Punk Singles Collection' (Anagram CD PUNK 13)

BUZZCOCKS

In February 1976, Manchester ex-student colleagues Pete Shelley and Howard Devoto drove a couple of hundred miles south to see gigs in High Wycombe and Welwyn Garden City by The Sex Pistols, having been intrigued by music press reports of the London punkers' on-stage musical energy and anarchy. Even more impressed after witnessing a show, they met Malcolm McLaren and offered to help him set up a Pistols gig in their home city. Back home, they also immediately set about putting together a Pistols-style band of their own, with the first Buzzcocks incarnation which was augmented by two friends, playing a debut gig in Bolton within two months of the High Wycombe expedition.

In June 1976, two Shelley/Devoto-promoted Pistols gigs took place, at Manchester's Lesser Free Trade Hall, and The Buzzcocks played their first gig of consequence at the foot of the support bill of the second, having recruited Steve Diggle (drums) and John Maher (drums) to join Howard (vocals) and Pete (vocals and guitar). They very quickly got into a gigging stride which saw their London debut in the August and a slot in the 100 Club Punk Festival in the September.

With no immediate record company interest, The Buzzcocks became one of the first punk bands to take the do-it-yourself route when they released the EP 'Spiral Scratch' on their own New Hormones label, with its initial 1000-copy pressing financed by loans from friends and families. The record had only been on the market for two weeks, however, when Devoto decided to leave, citing tiredness, poor health and a desire to get some college work done (although he would return to the music scene in 1978 with his own band Magazine). The band rapidly sorted themselves out and Shelley immediately became lead vocalist, Diggle moved to guitar, and early temporary member Garth Smith returned on bass, following which the band surged ahead as if nothing had happened.

August 1977 saw them signed by United Artists, though the first single with the label 'Orgasm Addict' suffered predictable airplay problems and was not a big seller, while during their first headlining tour in the November, Smith was fired for being too unreliable, and Steve Garvey took over as bass player. Beginning in February 1978 with 'What Do I Get', the band placed a rapid succession of snappy, driving singles in the national charts over the next two-and-a-half years, the biggest being 'Ever Fallen In Love (With Someone You Shouldnt've)' (later revived by Fine Young Cannibals) and 'Promises', which both made the Top 20. A trio of critically-rated albums followed – 'Another Music In A Different Kitchen', 'Love Bites' and 'A Different Kind Of Tension' – and were all UK Top 30 success stories in 1978-79.

In the early 80s, however, Shelley in particular began to tire of the round of touring and recording, and he split the band in February 1981, to re-emerge in short order as a solo performer, while at the same time Diggle also launched his own Buzzcocks-type band named Flag Of Convenience. Against the odds, however, the Buzzcocks would reform in 1989, this time adding former Smiths drummer Mike Joyce to the line-up during 1991, and finding new favour with fans almost a generation down the line from their punk origins.

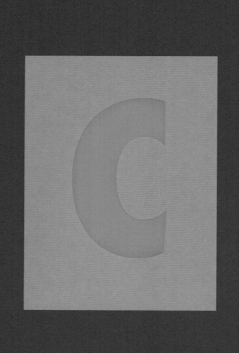

Cabaret Voltaire's Steve Mallinder

CABARET VOLTAIRE

This esoteric trio – Chris Watson (electronics and tapes), Richard H. Kirk (guitar and wind instruments) and Stephen Mallinder (bass and vocals) – formed in their native Sheffield in 1973/4, not as a band per se, but to record experimental tapes in an attic studio. The live debut came in May 1975, when, having talked themselves on to a local club stage, the trio were chased smartly off again by the extreme (violent, even) hostility of the audience to their decidedly lateral and non-listener-friendly music.

The advent two years later of the punk gig scene, with its associated removal of preconceived performance barriers and the wider audience acceptance of alienating sounds, put Cabaret Voltaire on a firmer footing for live performances, even though their electronic and mantra-based music had little in common with punk's simple, energetic nihilism as such. The indie label explosion which followed also gave the trio a chance for a record deal with an outfit unfettered by mainstream perceptions of what was musically viable. In 1978, after a one-off flirtation with Manchester's Factory Records, and multiple rejections from elsewhere, Rough Trade signed them on their own musical terms. This resulted in the approprately-named EP 'Extended Play ', followed the next year by the overtly punk influenced rock single 'Nag Nag Nag', and a debut album, 'Mix-Up,' which was essentially an electronic and tape loop collage.

The band began to hit the indie lists with singles like 'Silent Command' and 'Three Mantras', plus their next two albums, 'The Voice Of America' and 'Live At The YMCA', while their music began to point more solidly to the German-style Industrial genre, and then eventually into techno rhythmic sounds, which would solidify into a whole decade's subsequent work in, basically, experimental dance music. The flirtation with the punk scene which kick-started them was over by the early 80s, and certainly by the time Watson departed in October 1981 to leave the essence of Cabaret Voltaire as a (sometimes augmented) duo.

Recommended CD listening: 'The Voice Of America' (Mute CABS 2 CD)

Live on stage at CBGB's!
Left, The Ramones, and (below) Talking Heads

(left) CBGB's in all its jaded Bowery glory

CBGB's

Located at 315 Bowery, CBGB's, which was owned by Hilly Krystal, came to prominence in the mid-1970s as one of New York City's premiere club outlets for the new US wave of punk and alternative rock acts. From April 1974, it became a regular weekly venue for Tom Verlaine and Richard Hell's then-new band Television, and hot on this band's heels came The Stilettos (who metamorphosed a year or so later into Blondie), and – for their first gigs – The Ramones. Talking Heads also made their their live debut there (supporting the aforementioned Ramones), on June 20, 1975.

CBGB's was characterised by its tiny stage (about 10 feet square), and its long, narrow and dark environment. The club was immortalised on the compilation album 'Live At CBGB's', which was recorded there in June 1976, and featured a host of then-unsigned New York bands. Unlike many clubs of the period, CBGB's survived the disco era to still be operating as a live music venue into the 1980s.

Recommended CD listening: 'Live At CBGB's' (Atlantic 7567-82566-2)

CHAOS UK

A quartet from Bristol, Chaos UK were one of the first local bands to be signed, during 1982, to the city's own punk label Riot City (the name was a reference to Bristol itself during the St. Pauls riots of 1981), which had initially been formed as an outlet for fellow Bristolian punkers Vice Squad. Chaos UK's own name was similarly inspired by outside events: their lyrics were mostly angry responses to perceived social injustice and the general domestic ills of Britain in the early 1980s.

The band's forthright rants against society appeared on Riot City on a series of EPs: 'Burning Britain' included songs like 'Four Minute Warning' and 'Victimised', while 'Loud, Political And Uncompromising' (which more or less summed up the band itself) had numbers with such titles as 'No Security' and 'What About The Future'.

Unlike many of their contemporaries, Chaos UK did not wither and die when the Oi! movement imploded or punk's second wind ran out. As a socially and politically motivated band, they continued to find a role on both stage and record throughout the 80s and into the next decade, while musically also remaining remarkably faithful to their roots. Later albums included 'Enough To Make You Sick', 'Ear Slaughter' and 'Lawless Britain'.

Recommended CD listening: 'Total Chaos (The Singles Collection)' (Anagram Punk Collectors Series CD PUNK 26)

CHELSEA

Chelsea were formed in London in the late summer of 1976 by vocalist Gene October, who sought like-minded musicians through the traditional method of a *Melody Maker* small ad. Via this, he recruited drummer John Towe and bassist Tony James, who had got a day job after several months of foiled attempts to make a going concern of his and Mick Jones' outfit London S.S. Tony brought with him guitarist Billy Idol (nee William Broad), who had been one of the original 'Bromley Contingent' of Sex Pistols fans. The band rehearsed and even played a couple of gigs together (including a support slot for The Stranglers), but the line-up simply didn't gel, and at the end of November, the three instrumentalists handed October the group name and split – to form Generation X a fortnight later.

October did another round of recruiting, and by March 1977 had a new Chelsea (with James Stevenson on guitar, Henry Badowski on bass, and Carey Fortune on drums) on the road, and a deal with the fledgling Step Forward label, which released two stridently anti-establishment sides, 'Right To Work' and 'High Rise Living'. This aggregation also failed to work, however, and there was further disintegration in September, followed by yet another round of recruitment. Finally, by January 1978, October and Stevenson had brought in Dave Martin (guitar), Geoff Myles (bass) and Chris Bashford (drums), and this line-up eventually cut the band's first album 'Chelsea' again for Step Forward.

Commercial success consistently eluded Chelsea, which made it all the more surprising (as did their somewhat time-warped brand of carping 1977 punk) that they soldiered on through the 80s with a whole string of albums, gradually working their way through Miles Copeland's labels from Step Forward to Illegal and eventually I.R.S., for releases such as 'Alternative Hits', 'Rocks Off', 'Under Wraps' and 'Ultra Prophets'. The line-up changed several times through the decade, but always with vocalist October as the inevitable linchpin.

CHISWICK RECORDS

Launched in 1976 by record collector and dealer Ted Carroll, and based in London's Camden Town, Chiswick was one of the first of the new breed of small British independent labels which latched on to the burgeoning new wave of grassroots talent evident in the UK at the time. Its first releases (in addition to a reissue of Vince Taylor's 1960 classic 'Brand New Cadillac'), were by punky pub circuit bands like The Count Bishops, The Gorillas, and The 101'ers – the latter including guitarist Joe Strummer, who left to help launch The Clash just as his former band's sole Chiswick single 'Keys To Your Heart' was released.

Chiswick did well in low-overhead small label terms, but failed to have any major chart hits in its early years, although it was responsible for later punk collectibles like two singles by Skrewdriver, and 'Dead Vandals' by Scotland's Johnny & The Self-Abusers, who were infact an early incarnation of Simple Minds. But the label had its real commercial flowering in 1979, when it signed The Damned on their second time around (after losing Bryan James, splitting and then reforming), and gave the band its first Top 50 hit singles with 'Love Song', 'Smash It Up','I Just Can't Be Happy Today' and 'History Of The World (Part 1)'.

Chiswick eventually metamorphosed into Ace Records, one of the most prolific and highly-regarded reissue and specialist music outlets of the 1980s and 90s, but its original punk heritage is still reflected in a portion of its catalogue carrying the Big Beat logo.

Recommended CD listening: 'The Chiswick Story' (Chiswick CDWIK 2 100)

CHRON GEN

A quartet comprising Glynn Barber on vocals and guitar, John Thurlow on guitar, Pete Dimmock on bass and John Johnson on drums, Chron Gen were first formed in January 1978, but didn't arrive on record until punk got its second wind in the UK during the Oi! days of the early 1980s. In the summer of 1981, the band issued a four-track EP titled 'Puppets Of War' on their own Gargoyle label (including the song 'Chronic Generation' from which they had abridged their own name), and this led to a one-off deal with Small Wonder Records for the follow-up single 'Reality', which proceeded to make the indie charts. They found nationwide exposure on the Apocalypse Punk package tour, playing alongside Anti-Pasti, Discharge and The Exploited, and were then signed early in 1982 by Secret Records, the punk-orientated indie label which already had the likes of The Business and The Exploited. A revival of the Captain Sensible oldie 'Jet Boy, Jet Girl' followed, plus one track – 'Clouded Eyes' – on the wittily-titled 'Britannia Waives The Rules' EP, alongside Infa Riot and The Exploited. Secret also released Chron Gen's only album, 'Chronic Generation Oi, No1' in mid-1982.

THE CIRCLE JERKS

The four-man Circle Jerks were formed in Los Angeles in 1980 by Keith Morris, previously the vocalist with fellow L.A. punk band Black Flag. The initial line-up was completed by Greg Hetson (ex-Redd Kross) on guitar, Roger Rogerson on bass, and Lucky Lehrer on drums. The band ploughed a very similar furrow to Black Flag: an uncompromisingly harsh, attacking sound with suitably disenfranchised and ranting lyrics. Their first album 'Group Sex' recorded for the Frontier label, appeared in February 1981, while four additional recordings – tracks like 'Red Tape' and 'Back Against The Wall' – appeared on Slash Records' L.A. punk anthology 'The Decline Of Western Civilisation' alongside similar material by X, Fear, Black Flag and others, and the next couple of years saw further appearances on other similar hardcore-orientated compilation albums, notably The Alternative Tentacles set 'Let Them Eat Jellybeans', put together by The Dead Kennedys' Jello Biafra. The second Circle Jerks album proper was 'Wild In The Streets,' released by Faulty Products early in 1982.

Ever purveyors of an alternative noise and attitude, The Circle Jerks were not destined to sniff any mainstream commercial success, but their enduring popularity as a gigging attraction with the West Coast alternative audiences ensured them longevity through the 1980s with little change of style, though Rogerson and Lehrer were replaced along the way by Zander Scloss and Adolph Clark. Further albums by The Circle Jerks included 'Golden Shower' in 1983, and 'V1' in 1987.

Recommended CD listening: 'Group Sex' (Weird Systems WS 031 YZ)

Top, Chelsea with Tony James and Billy Idol
Centre, Chelsea's Gene October
Bottom left, Chron Gen
Bottom right, Cockney Rejects

The Clash

The Clash were arguably the most musically accomplished act, with the clearest vision of what they were about and where they were going, to emerge from the melee of the original London punk explosion in 1976. The band evolved out of guitarist/vocalist Mick Jones' abortive attempts with Tony James to make something of their sprawling rehearsal band The London S.S., which had hovered on the verge of getting its act together through most of 1975. By the spring of the following year, Jones had seen the writing on the wall, and departed the band along with the non-playing but entrepreneural Bernie Rhodes, who was soon to become The Clash's manager. They recruited two sometime London S.S.-ers, drummer Terry Chimes and Paul Simonon, who had previously auditioned as a vocalist, but was persuaded by Jones to learn the bass if he wanted the gig. Guitarist Keith Levine, known to both Jones and Simonon, rounded out a basic band framework, but Rhodes had his eye on another key musician who was also known to be a songwriter, and approached Joe Strummer (real name John Mellor), the vocalist and guitarist with the 101-ers, a fairly successful pub R&B band. Strummer agreed to join, and The Clash were born, adopting the name at Simonon's suggestion (he kept seeing the word in the *Evening Standard*) after they had considered more exotic possibilities including The Weak Heart Drops and The Psych Negatives.

In June 1976 the newly-formed band hauled themselves and their equipment to a deserted warehouse in London's Camden Town, which they made habitable and christened Rehearsal Rehearsals. It became both their HQ and a residential squat for several of the members, and two months of solid rehearsal ensued there, until on August 29 The Clash played their first public gig at Islington's Screen On The Green cinema, supporting The Sex Pistols. Almost immediately, however, Levene decided to leave (he would eventually resurface alongside John Lydon in PiL), and was not replaced. As a quartet, the band then played at the 100 Club Punk Festival in September, and an offer to join The Pistols on their Anarchy In The UK tour followed. This was accepted, but the jaunt quickly became a farce as date after date was cancelled in a sudden – partly press encouraged – public epidemic of cold feet over 'punk hooliganism'.

By the beginning of 1977, the band were headlining their own dates, and recorded a five-song demo session of original Jones and Strummer songs with producer Guy Stevens at Polydor's studio, only to hit another setback in March when Chimes – who by his own admission did not see eye-to-eye with the band's political stance and general idealism, decided to leave. Nonetheless, he agreed to stay a while for recording sessions after Rhodes announced that, following a lengthy tug-of-war between Polydor and CBS, the band had secured a deal with the latter. With businesslike haste, they recorded the 'White Riot' single and their debut album 'The Clash', which CBS rush-released within a week of each other. The single made No.38 in the chart, and the album reached No.12, in a four-month chart residency. Curiously, CBS' parent company in the US declared that

the album was 'too unfinished' for American ears, and didn't give it a US release, setting it up to become the country's biggest-selling rock import ever, with an estimated 100,000 British copies sold on the back of college radio, rock press and specialist dealer support.

After extensive auditioning of drummers, Nicky 'Topper' Headon, whose heart was actually in jazz and soul rhythms, but who had played briefly with Jones in The London S.S., joined to fill the gap left by Chimes, and the classic Clash line-up was complete. Their second single 'Remote Control', chosen by CBS and released in June against the band's wishes, failed to chart, but their riposte with 'Complete Control', cut with Jamaican producer Lee Perry, made No.18 in October. All through the year they toured heavily, both around the UK and on the continent, and there were more than a few incidents (not to mention brushes with the law) to later remember these days on the road for. At least two British gigs, one in the summer and another just prior to Christmas, descended into old-fashioned rock'n'roll audience riots – a sure sign, were one now needed, that The Clash were (while The Sex Pistols were busy disintegrating in the 'States) now fully-fledged stars in the punk-rock firmament.

1978 saw more touring, medium-sized UK hit singles with 'Clash City Rockers', '(White Man) In Hammersmith Palais' and 'Tommy Gun' (the latter their first top 20 hit), plus a No.2 success in November with the second album 'Give 'Em Enough Rope', the band's first major recording project to feature Headon on drums. Recorded in both London and the US, it had an unlikely (though in the event, successful) choice of producer, in Sandy Pearlman of Blue Oyster Cult fame. This set was passed for release by US CBS, and reached a modest No.128 early in 1979. The other major event of 1978, just before the LP's release, was the dismissal of Bernie Rhodes, following increasing manager/band difficulties.

In 1979, although they spent much time touring in the US, where they made a major name for themselves as a concert attraction, as well as enjoying the buzz of sharing stages with personal favourites old and new (Bo Diddley, Screaming Jay Hawkins, Joe Ely, The Cramps), the band scored three UK hit singles with 'English Civil War', the EP 'The Cost Of Living' (led by a revival of the Bobby Fuller Four favourite 'I Fought The Law'), and 'London Calling', which was their most successful single to date, reaching No.11. The latter was also the title track of their third album, a double set produced by Guy Stevens which received widespread critical acclaim. It hit No.9 at the tail-end of the year, and was also their first major US seller, climbing to No.27 in the Spring of 1980. The American-only single release 'Train In Vain (Stand By Me)' also peaked at No.23 there at the same time.

March 1980 saw the release of the movie *Rude Boy*, much of which had been filmed around The Clash's touring activities over the previous year, and was a part-documentary and part fictional account of the life of band roadie Ray Gange. They also toured and recorded with Jamaican DJ

Mikey Dread, with whom they had the joint hit single 'Bankrobber', which reached No.12 in the UK. Considerable time was also spent in the studio in the US on recordings for the next album, which, with an over-abundance of material in the can, eventually appeared at the end of the year as the triple LP Sandanista!. Even with the band taking reduced royalties so that it could be sold at double-album price, the release still stretched the pockets of some of the fans (and was panned by critics, who felt the self-produced set disappointing and self-indulgent), and only made No.19 in the UK, while climbing to 24 in the US.

At the beginning of 1981, Bernie Rhodes returned to the management reins at Strummer's request, and old difficulties seemed forgotten as he orchestrated successful Clash tours all over the world, including US, UK and European treks during 1991, a Japanese tour and other Pacific Rim territory dates early in 1982, more British and Euro dates in the spring of that year, and two major US tours through most of the rest of it, including one supporting The Who. An upheaval occurred during May 1982, though, when, after completing the sessions for the next album, 'Combat Rock', Headon decided to quit (citing 'political differences'); he was replaced on the aforementioned US treks by a hastily-recalled Chimes.

'Combat Rock' became the biggest-selling Clash album yet, reaching No.2 in the UK and No.7 in the United States, and also spun off a couple of notable hit singles in 'Should I Stay Or Should I Go?' and the Topper Headon composition 'Rock The Casbah', which only made No.30 in Britain, but went all the way to No.8 across the Atlantic. A new full-time drummer, Pete Howard, took over from Terry Chimes in May 1983, and with the line-up seemingly secure once again, and the achievement of such widespread commercial success, The Clash should have been riding on top of the world.

It was not to be, however. Tensions between Joe Strummer and Mick Jones had been escalating for some time, and their differences reached a bitter climax in September 1983 when Jones' departure was announced by Strummer and Simonon. He was to re-emerge a year or so later at the head of new outfit Big Audio Dynamite, while in The Clash he was replaced in January 1984 by two new guitarists, Vince White and Nick Sheppard. A busy gigging schedule ensued through 1984 and 1985, but the creative heart of the band was proved to have been sundered when this final line-up recorded its one and only album, 'Cut The Crap'. Critics zeroed in on the latter word, and even many previously loyal fans found

the collection lacklustre: it briefly made the No.16 slot in the UK chart, then vanished out of sight. Strummer and Simonon decided that enough was enough, and after a final, low-key 'busking' British tour, they broke up the band once and for all.

Strummer's later career would include several movie acting roles, plus assorted musical projects which even included a spell singing with The Pogues. Isolated musical activities by Simonon and Headon made rather less impact. The music of The Clash, however, would not lie down. A hits compilation album, 'The Story Of The Clash, Volume 1', made No.7 during 1988, with 'I Fought The Law', taken from it as a single, reaching No.24. The band's most spectacular posthumous success, however, was to come in 1991 when 'Should I Stay Or Should I Go', from the 'Combat Rock' album, was used on a British television commercial for Levi's jeans. The reissued single soared to No.1 (and became the band's biggest-ever UK seller) as a result. Rumours that Jones, Strummer, Simonon and Headon would reunite on the back of this success were rife for a while, but in the event a reunion did not occur.

Recommended CD listening: 'The Story Of The Clash, Volume 1' (Columbia 460244 2), and 'Clash On Broadway' (3-CD box set) (Epic/Legacy 46991)

PUNK!

COCK SPARRER

Along with Jimmy Pursey's Sham 69, this band from London's East End were the first to use punk as an anthem for working class expressionism specific to the capital. However, unlike those of Pursey, Cock Sparrer's somewhat lumpen and laboured efforts brought them little success and scarcely more than scorn from the critics (an *NME* review disparagingly called their first single 'punk by numbers').

The quintet, comprising Colin McFaull (vocals), Mick Beaufey (guitar), Garrie Lammin (guitar), Steve Burgess (bass) and Charlie Bruce (drums) started out as a pre-punk pub band in 1974, attracting a largely skinhead audience which they retained after speeding up into punk mode after the advent of The Sex Pistols. After playing support to Motorhead and the reformed Small Faces, the band was signed by the unlikely major Decca records, a label fast running out of creative steam after decades of glory, but as eager as any other in 1977 to get itself a slice of punk action. However, Decca, predictably, had little idea of what to do with its new signing, and chart glory was not about to come Cock Sparrer's way. Their debut single 'Runnin' Riot' was a bolshy skinhead anthem with a photo of a football pitch invasion on its limited-run picture sleeve – musical and visual images which anticipated the boot-boy Oi! movement destined to drive British punk through the first couple of years of the 80s, and, unfortunately, both four years ahead of their time. Bizarrely, the band revived The Rolling Stones' 'We Love You' for their follow-up, though its B-side, 'Chip On My Shoulder', was probably more appropriate to their situation.

After the Decca deal (and, indeed, Decca) fizzled out, the band went to Carrere Records in 1982 for 'England Belongs To Me'— a single which proved to be a further miscalculation when it was taken up as an anthem by right-wing skinheads of the racist, swastika-toting variety, who suddenly dominated their audiences. Appalled, the essentially non-political quintet closed up operations for a while in an effort to distance themselves from the neo-Nazis and from the violence beginning to mar those punk gigs which attracted right-wing activists. Their credentials should have presented them as ideal leaders of the Oi! scene, but their career-long bad luck made sure that movement would, in fact, kill them off. A couple of comeback releases on the Syndicate and Razor labels later in the 1980s only proved conclusively that their moment had passed.

COCKNEY REJECTS

Formed, as indicated by their name, in East London in 1978, The Cockney Rejects adopted the concept of punk-as-London-anthem previously the plot of Sham 69 and Cock Sparrer. The band were a quartet of devoted West Ham Utd fans, comprising Stinky Turner on vocals, Mickey Geggus (Stinky's brother) on guitar, Vance Riorden (formerly of The Dead Flowers) on bass, and Andy Scott (previously with The Tickets) on drums.

Initially offered a one-single deal by Small Wonder on the strength of a demo tape, they persuaded Sham 69's Jimmy Pursey to produce the three-track single 'Flares And Slippers', which quickly sold out its initial 5,000 pressing in the summer of 1979 and was instrumental in securing the band a deal with EMI. This led to a string of six hit singles within a hectic 12-month period, beginning with 'I'm Not A Fool', and peaking with 'The Greatest Cockney Rip-Off' (a sly dig at mentor Pursey), which only missed the top 20 by one position. Three albums, with the tongue-in-cheek titles of 'Greatest Hits Vol.1', 'Greatest Hits Vol.2' and 'Greatest Hits Vol.3' (even though none of them were compilations as such, and the third was a live set), were equally successful, all finding Top 30 success between March 1980 and April 1981.

Because the majority of their material was a sort of musical variation on the football hooligan chant, combining yobbish assertiveness with anti-establishment gripes (like 'Police Car'), The Rejects became role models for the burgeoning Oi! movement, but as the early 80s wore on, they took something of a back seat (at least in terms of media exposure) to Oi! bands like The 4-Skins and Infa Riot, who had more of a penchant for doing those gigs where unrest and violence brewed. When it came down to it, The Cockney Rejects actually felt most at home as part of the crowd on the Upton Park terraces, as their Top 40 rendition of the West Ham anthem 'I'm Forever Blowing Bubbles' attests.

Recommended CD listening: 'The Best Of The Cockney Rejects' (Dojo CD 82)

JOHN COOPER CLARKE

One of two poets (the other being Patrik Fitzgerald) to surface within the idiom of the first British punk era, John Cooper Clarke, from Salford, Manchester, must also qualify as one of rock's first rappers, a machine-gun 'hip' delivery predating by several years that staccato words-and-rhythm meld which would come to full prominence in the 1980s.

Clarke began his poetry readings in the early 70s in local folk clubs, and as an adjunct to his short-lived stand-up comedy act on the Northern club circuit. Developing a visual image cloned from Bob Dylan circa 'Highway 61 Revisited', he added music to some of his dates through a collaboration with a Manchester band named the Ferretts, and became

PUNK!

Opposite: Cock Sparrer
This page: John Cooper Clarke

entwined with the Northern punk fraternity when, in October 1977, he served as support act for a Buzzcocks gig at Manchester's Electric Circus (recorded for Virgin's 'Short Circuit' compilation album), and recorded an EP for Tosh Ryan's local indie label Rabid, which was produced by Martin Hannet and included the two parts of his alliterative word avalanche 'Psycle Sluts'.

February 1978 brought a major recording deal with Epic, and in September came his first album 'Disguise In Love' (note the word play pun), which was again produced by Hannett and featured guest appearances by Be-Bop Deluxe's Bill Nelson and the Buzzcocks' Pete Shelley. Though both this and the mid-1979 10-inch live album 'Walking Back To Happiness' failed to make the charts, Cooper Clarke did crack the Top 40 in March 1979 with his single 'Gimmix! play Loud' – which, with its triangular coloured vinyl limited edition pressing, was certainly not lacking a gimmick or two itself.

In 1980, Clarke represented Britain in the first World Poetry Olympics, held in Westminster Abbey's Poets' Corner, and also finally racked up a hit album with 'Snap, Crackle And Bop' (containing his best-known piece 'Beasley Street'), which made No.26, and was followed by a co-headlining UK tour with former Penetration lead singer Pauline Murray's band The Invisible Girls (who had backed him on the LP).

Clarke also published two books of poetry, *The Cooper Clarke Directory* and *Ten Years In An Open-Neck Shirt*, before allowing the recording side of his career to wind down after a further album, 'Zip Style Method', charted briefly in 1982. He almost dropped out of visibility later in the 80s when he set up home with former Velvet Underground singer Nico, but since the chanteuse's death has re-emerged performing on the 'alternative' club circuit, albeit with a less commercial profile than in his Punk Poet glory years.

Recommended CD listening: 'Snap, Crackle & Bop' (Columbia Rewind 477380-2)

ELVIS COSTELLO

Although Elvis Costello was never part of the core punk movement or style as such, the early part of his career is inextricably linked with it in several ways. Firstly, he appeared on the scene at the same time as the early UK punk bands, and the fact that he was thus perceived as part of an overall innovative new wave helped him get both media coverage and record company commitment – he signed to Stiff within four months of The Damned. Secondly, the fact that Costello rapidly found wide (international, even) acceptance as a writer/performer with a sharp new agenda served as a catalyst and role model for other creative individuals who were at first more easily defined by punk's constraints, but whose ambitions included broader songwriting and musical horizons – John Lydon, The Clash, Paul Weller and The Buzzcocks' Pete Shelley, to name but a few. The closest concessions to punk on Costello's 1977 debut album 'My Aim Is True' was the occasional anger in its mostly short, sharp songs (an emotion he would hone expertly in later work), and the fact that he had short hair and a baleful stare in the sleeve photo – but he proved very early on you could be halfway to mainstream appeal and acclaim, but still have attitude. Psychologically, that was extremely important to punk as a whole.

Recommended CD listening: 'My Aim Is True' (Demon DPAM 1) and 'This Year's Model' (Demon DPAM 2)

Crass bass player Pete Wright with vocalist Steve Ignorant

CRASS

Anarchist thinkers and musicians Penny Rimbaud (who played drums) and Steve Ignorant (vocalist) formed Crass – originally a duo – in 1978, as a musical offshoot of the general radical activities conducted from Rimbaud's farmhouse at North Weald, Essex, which for several years had been home to a large, open commune of around a dozen like-minded souls. By its very co-operative nature, the rest of this commune generated input into the band, which very quickly expanded its ranks to include Eve Libertine (vocals), Joy De Vivre (vocals), Phil Free (lead guitar), Andy Palmer (rhyhtm guitar), G (piano and flute) and Pete Wright (bass). Film maker Mick Duffield also frequently provided a backdrop to their live performances.

After a live debut at a squatters' free festival, Crass got a one-off deal in January 1979 with Small Wonder Records to release 'The Feeding Of The 5,000', a 12-inch EP with an unlikely 17 tracks – which immediately reduced to 16 when no pressing plant would agree to manufacture it because of objections to the opening track 'Asylum'. In order to get the record released at all, the band deleted it and replaced the track with a two-minute silence which they entitled 'Free Speech'.

Bruised by their encounter with the institutions of the real world, the commune took the obvious alternative route, and launched their own Crass label, on which the remainder of their repertoire appeared. Crass Records were characterised by DIY artwork, photocopied sleeves which doubled as anarchist broadsheets, and a unique catalogue numbering system that involved a countdown to 1984 – clearly a year of symbolic significance to the band with its Orwellian connotations. Strongly political singles like 'Reality Asylum', 'Bloody Revolution', 'Nagasaki Nightmare' and 'How Does It feel To Be The Mother Of 1,000 Dead?' (a 'tribute' to Margaret Thatcher) performed extremely well in the indie charts over the next three years, as did the albums 'Stations Of The Cross', 'Penis Envy' and 'Christ The Album' (all titles which ensured that they were very rarely stocked by the mainstream High Street record chains).

The Crass label, and indirectly the band, was ironically terminated by financial realities – in a desire to sell their product at rock-bottom prices, the commune had overlooked the need to charge VAT, as required by law, and found themselves saddled with an almighty revenue bill. While they lasted, however, Crass probably lived and espoused the minimalist punk lifestyle more than any other band before or since.

Recommended CD listening: 'Stations Of The Cross' (Crass 521984 CD)

D

The Damned

Over a period of nearly 20 years, The Damned have become something of a British musical institution – a future which would have seemed most unlikely at the time of their formation, which took place in May 1976 as part of the very genesis of the British punk movement.

The initial group was a trio, comprising guitarist Brian James, bassist Captain Sensible (or Ray Burns, as his parents knew him), and drummer Rat Scabies (real name Chris Miller). James and Scabies had both played previously with hometown bands and with the proto-punk outfit London SS, while Sensible had been a guitarist with Johnny Moped. These three first grouped as part of the pickup backing band accompanying *NME* writer-turned-rocker Nick Kent as the Subterraneans, but a couple of gigs with Kent were enough to assure the trio that they had a better future in their own right, and a vocal frontman was quickly recruited in the form of Dave Vanian, otherwise gainfully employed as a gravedigger in Hemel Hempstead. Vanian (real name Letts), who sported a look like an on-call extra from a Dracula movie, proved to be the ideal visual focus for the band – a million miles from Johnny Rotten, but equally hard to look away from. Along with the irrepressible Sensible – who generally wasn't, and adopted the Keith Moon approach to getting oneself noticed in a crowd – he made the early Damned a compelling act to witness.

After six weeks of noisy rehearsals around London, the new four-piece band eventually debuted live on July 6, at London's 100 club, supporting The Sex Pistols, who had already been gigging for seven months, and who were at least partial role models for The Damned (and just about every other new band in London at the time).

Things moved fairly quickly for The Damned once they started gigging

in earnest. An excursion to the Mont Du Marsan punk festival in the south of France during the summer of 1976 introduced them (via a fight on the bus, allegedly), to rocker-of-all-trades Nick Lowe, who in turn took them to the fledgling independent label Stiff Records. Produced by Lowe, The Damned's first single (and Stiff's sixth) 'New Rose' was released on October 22, and remains a milestone as the first official release by any British punk band. Though it failed to chart – possibly because of Stiff's lack of distribution push in its early days – the music press feted the single, and the band went from strength to strength as a live act. Leaving – or being pushed – early from their support slot on The Sex Pistols' troubled 'Anarchy' tour of the UK at the end of the year did them no harm, and they created further new firsts in April 1977, when they became the first UK punk band to play in America (including a gig at the New York punk mecca CBGB's), and the first to release an album ('Damned, Damned, Damned', produced again by Lowe) and get it into the UK charts, where it reached a not unimpressive No.34.

After several months of busy, successful touring (occasionally marred by disturbance and violence from anti-punk elements), and a couple more Stiff singles which oddly still refused to chart, some blips began to appear in The Damned game plan in the second half of 1977. Brian James insisted that a second guitarist, in the shape of Robert 'Lu' Edmonds, was added to 'fatten' the sound, but not without some misgivings on behalf of the rest of the band. Disagreements then arose over the production of a second album, with the job eventually falling into the unlikely hands of Nick Mason from Pink Floyd. Titled 'Music For Pleasure', this second release, perhaps

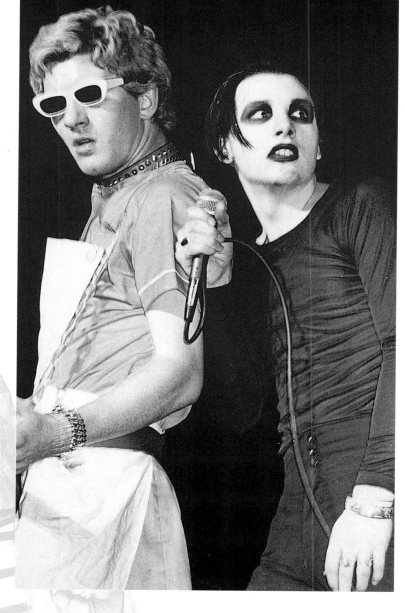

Neat Neat Damned

significantly, didn't chart. A clearly disillusioned Scabies departed the ranks as soon as the LP was completed (Jon Moss, later drummer with Culture Club, replaced him), and set a rapid path of disintegration into progress. James was the next to go (to form Tanz Der Youth), in February 1978, and within weeks, the rest of the band decided to throw in the towel as well: the complete line-up regrouped for a one-off farewell concert at the Rainbow Theatre in London, at the end of which their equipment was symbolically smashed up. By this time, The Sex Pistols' line-up had also fractured, with a departed Johnny Rotten becoming John Lydon of PiL, and the initial British punk movement was in an advanced state of absorbtion into the wider music scene, sprouting new green shoots in the more musicianly guise of 'new wave'.

Against general expectations, though, there was to be a part 2 to The Damned story – the first of several returns from the dead which would be the key to the band's mutation and eventual survival into the 1990s. Though much of the later career, and the myriad line-up changes it involved, lies outside the scope of this book, the first resurrection brought them right back to the heart of punk – indeed, as one of the last major bastions of its original uncompromising style. Vanian, Scabies and Sensible first regrouped in September of 1978, with the Captain now on guitar. Lemmy from Motorhead filled in on bass for their first gig, to be replaced for a while by Henry Badowski, formerly of Chelsea, and eventually on a full-time basis by Algy Ward, who had previously been with the Saints. Things were initially kept tentative: they toured as 'The Doomed' until they were sure of legal ownership of their previous name (it was bought back

from Brian James, who had originally registered it), and a couple of singles were almost under-the-counter affairs. Early 1979 real resurrection, and with it commercial success, as the band signed a new deal with Stiff's old (friendly) rival Chiswick, and scored three UK chart hits in a row with 'Love Song', 'Smash It Up' and 'I Just Can't Be Happy Today', also charting with the LP 'Machine Gun Etiquette', from which all the singles were taken. This material was high-energy punk rock at its creative and commercial peak – 'Smash It Up' perhaps being one of the genre's definitive statements – and was also traditional British punk's virtual last gasp in the the marketplace; the music was splintering around The Damned in a myriad indie, hardcore and avant-punk directions. The band themselves would never quite be the same musical unit again, and their eventual highly successful chart career in the late 1980s would show them as a keenly–honed pop band making successful revivals of Love's 'Alone Again Or' and Barry Ryan's 'Eloise'. When punk was king, though, the Damned were truly princes.

Recommended CD listening: 'Skip Off School, To See The Damned' (The Stiff Singles A's And B's) (Demon VEXCD 12)

'The Best Of The Damned': 'Another Great Compact Disc From The Damned' (Big Beat CDDAM 1)

THE DEAD BOYS

Formed in Cleveland, Ohio, in 1975, The Dead Boys – disciples of the New York Dolls and Iggy Pop's Stooges – became one of the mainstays of the CBGB's club new wave scene when they moved to New York around a year after first coming together (and six months after first splitting up.) The line-up was Iggy Pop-worshipper Stiv Bators on vocals, Cheetah Chrome (Gene O'Connor) and Jimmy Zero on guitars, Jeff Magnum on bass and Johnny Blitz (John Madansky) on drums, and they were originally known as Frankenstein, in which manifestation they had played just a handful of early gigs in Cleveland.

A year into their New York reincarnation, the band were signed by Sire Records, and released their debut album 'Young, Loud And Snotty' in October 1977, followed eight months later by the provocatively-titled 'We Have Come For Your Children'. Neither set was a particularly big seller, and a couple of months after the release of their second LP, wearied by the stress of the New York punk circuit (where violence was apparently rife at, and after, their gigs), The Dead Boys called it a day – though they would reconvene for occasional one-offs during the early 80s; infact one such appearance in 1981 was recorded for Bomp Records' live album 'Night Of The Living Dead Boys'.

Bators remained the most musically active ex-Dead Boy after the split, first briefly with the Stiv Bators Band in California and The Wanderers in London, and then, from September 1981, with the UK-based Lords Of The New Church, a band which he formed with former Damned member Brian James, and Dave Treganna, previously of Sham 69.

DEAD KENNEDYS

Internationally, San Francisco's Dead Kennedys were probably the most controversial of all punk bands aside from The Sex Pistols. For a start, their name was never likely to endear them to any part of established America, and at one point, the band joked (albeit semi-seriously) that they got as many death threats as fan mail!

The Kennedys were formed early in 1978, in a line-up comprising Jello Biafra (vocals), East Bay Ray (guitar), Klaus Flouride (bass) and Bruce Slesinger (drums). Their first single, 'California Uber Alles', appeared in 1979 on their own Alternative Tentacles label in the US, and via the Scottish indie Fast Product in the UK. The song, which proved that the band had started much as they wished to go on, was a forthright rant against California's then-governor Jerry Brown, suggesting that his liberal stance was a facade for unbridled power-seeking. Few friends were won, either, with the follow-up 'Holiday In Cambodia', whose title tells its own story.

These two singles, though, were big sellers in the British indie market – when the first UK Indie Chart was published, in February 1980, both were in the Top 30, several months after release in the case of 'California Uber Alles'. The second single was on Cherry Red, which signed the Kennedys to a UK deal and started to promote them heavily, to the effect that both next single, 'Kill The Poor' (another establishment-friendly slogan!) and their debut album 'Fresh Fruit For Rotting Vegetables,' each released in the Autumn of 1980, made the UK pop charts.

Lead singer Biafra put his money where his mouth had led, as it were, when elections came up for a new Mayor of San Francisco. Campaigning

DELTA 5

Formed in Leeds in September 1978, the Delta 5 were a five piece that comprised Juiz Sale (vocals and guitar), Bethan Peters (vocals and bass), Alan Rigs (guitar), Roz Allen (bass) and Kelvin Knight (drums). The band coalesced in an initially low-key fashion on what was known as Leeds' 'funk/punk' scene, aided and frequently abetted in the early months by members of the Mekons (on whose debut single Roz had played) and The Gang Of Four, whose musical influence they also acknowledged.

Eventually signed to Rough Trade, the band released their first single 'Mind Your Own Business' in December 1979, but it was the follow-up 'Anticipation,' early the following year, which was their best seller, making the indie chart. They fairly quickly outgrew their punk influences, however, particularly after two-thirds of the original members left concurrently with a shift to the Pre label. This sojourn produced their only album, 'See The Whirl', but interest in it was minimal, and the revised line-up decided to call it a day during 1981.

on a light-hearted ticket designed to highlight the bullshitting of his various opponents, Biafra came up against nine other candidates – and emerged at a creditable fourth position in the poll!

More controversy erupted in the Spring of 1981, when the band released the deliberately outrageously-titled single 'Too Drunk To Fuck'. Subject to a total radio ban everywhere in the world (and even legal action against shops selling it, in a few instances), it was nonetheless their biggest seller yet, reaching No.36 in the UK singles chart. This was, however, the peak of The Kennedys' commercial success: the second album 'Plastic Surgery Disasters' (on which D.H. Peligro replaced Slesinger on drums) made only the indie charts in the UK, as would later sets like 'Frankenchrist' (which precipitated a legal action over alleged obscenity) and 'Bedtime For Democracy' in the mid-80s, and also such singles as the typically provocative 'Nazi Punks Fuck Off'.

The band continued to record sporadically throughout the 80s, though disbanded before the end of the decade. Biafra also made several solo albums, both during the band's tenure and afterwards, later examples of which have anthologised his political speeches rather than music. Pulled more and more into radical politics by his uncompromising stand on a number of heartfelt topics, the vocalist became an active crusader against censorship, aligning himself with Frank Zappa and similar establishment-baiters in the entertainment world.

Recommended CD listening: 'Fresh Fruit For Rotting Vegetables' (Cherry Red CDBRED 10)

Opposite, Stiv Bators (right) on stage at CBGB's
Above, anathema to middle America, The Dead Kennedys

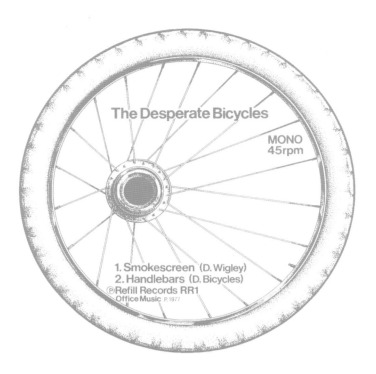

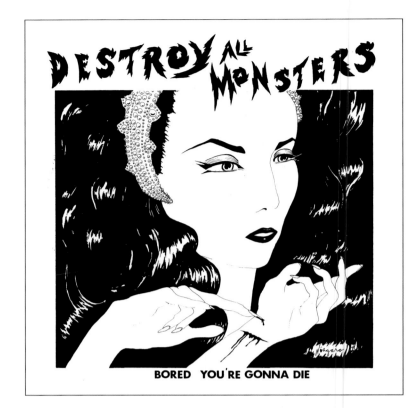

DESPERATE BICYCLES

Formed in Dalston, East London during March 1977, The Desperate Bicycles were one of the first bands to seriously aspire to the 'Do It Yourself' recording ethic which was to mushroom by the end of the decade into the British indie label scene. The band, originally comprising Danny Wigley on vocals, Nicky Stephens on keyboards, his brother Roger Stephens on bass, and Dave Papworth on drums, formed the Refill label in August 1977 to release their first single 'Smokescreen'. Costing a princely £153 to record, manufacture (500 copies) and package, the disc was pressed as a rather unconventional EP, in that it repeated the same two songs, 'Smokescreen' and 'Handlebars', on both sides – an idiosyncrasy repeated six months later on the equally D.I.Y. follow-up, 'The Medium Was Tedium/Don't Back The Front' (the latter song an early punk backlash against the right-wing elements which were frequently intent on claiming it for subversive ends.) The band pressed 1000 copies of this disc, using the profits generated by its predecessor. The band never troubled the charts, but their sales were obviously sufficient to keep the Refill label self-financing (with each release effectively subsidising the next one), and it managed a total of six Desperate Bicycles singles up to mid-1980, plus an additional release by The Evening Outs. The original band, however, only stayed the course for the first couple of singles: by 1980, Wigley was the only first-generation survivor, teamed with guitarist Dan Electro and drummer Jeff Titley, and by the following year, this trio too had split.

DESTROY ALL MONSTERS

With a name taken from a Japanese trash-monster movie, this Detroit-based group had existed in loose form for some three years with guitarist Cary Loren and ex-model and graphic artist vocalist Niagara (real name Lynn Rovner) as its core, when the arrival in 1977 of former Stooges guitarist Ron Asheton, plus sax player Ben Miller and his brother Larry on additional guitar, galvanised them into a higher profile just in time to intercept the arrival of punk on the US club scene. Early in 1978, they recorded a debut single, coupling 'Bored' and 'You're Gonna Die', on their own indie label. The UK rights to this were picked up 'blind' by the new independent Cherry Red Records, on the strength of an article on the band in *Sounds*, accompanied by an impressive pic of Niagara. Cherry Red's Ian McNay paid only $500 for the licence, but saw his instinct pay off when the British release sold an impressive 7,000 copies.

Mid-1979 saw another stellar addition to the ranks in the shape of bassist Mike Davis, formerly of the MC5. Drummer Ron King came in around the same time, while the Miller brothers and original guitarist Loren departed the fold. Cherry Red financed a UK visit by the band, but their London gigs were somewhat ramshackle, and gained savage rock press reviews, which effectively ended their honeymoon with the British punk audience – later singles 'Meet The Creeper' and 'What Do I Get' aroused comparatively little interest. Following a couple more own-label releases in the States, including a live EP, the band split, with Asheton moving on to form New Race with one-time MC5 colleague Dennis Thompson. Cary Loren and Ben and Larry Miller also tried again in 1980 with a group named Xanadu, but found no commercial success.

Recommended CD listening: 'Bored' (Cherry Red CDMRED 94)

'Are We Not Men?' – a good question

DEVO

From Akron, Ohio, Devo were an example of the many energetic new wave bands on both sides of the Atlantic who came to notice in the mid-1970s as part of the punk perception, but who quite quickly departed the parameters of the genre for their own eccentric musical path. Curiously, though, Devo's own deliberate eccentricity – their constant sloganeering about the philosophy of 'De-Evolution', (triumphant return to the basic, the seminal and the non-virtuoso) – precisely mirrored what punk, in a wider context, stood for in relation to the music of the 70s rock mainstream. In that sense, the band were punks in a very real way.

Devo, whose original line-up consisted of Mark Mothersbaugh (vocals), his brothers Bob and Tim Mothersbaugh (guitar and drums), and Jerry Casale (bass), were up and gigging in Ohio some time before The Sex Pistols played their first gig on the other side of the Atlantic, and this early live work shook out the personnel – drummer Alan Myers replaced Jim Mothersbaugh, and Bob Casale (Jerry's brother) was added on keyboards. Their quirky, gonzoid stage image and antics (delivering the De-Evolution manifesto) tended to enthuse and alienate their audiences in roughly equal proportions – coincidentally, just like The Sex Pistols. Their debut, the small label single 'Jocko Homo'/'Mongoloid', seemed willfully moronic to US audiences when issued in America at the end of 1976; significantly, when given a UK release by Stiff Records early in 1978, with punk established commercially, it was a chart success – one of four in quick succession.

1978 also saw Devo signed by two major labels, Warner Bros. in the US and Virgin in Britain. The band also released their first album in the same year, 'Are We Not Men? – We Are Devo' (the tag line from 'Jocko Homo'), which went further towards establishing them musically on both sides of the Atlantic. However, by late 1980, when 'Whip It' finally gave them a big American hit (and a final British one), snappy electronic dance rhythms had taken the place of their back-to-basics rock: evolution, it seemed, had caught up with them after all.

Recommended CD listening: 'Hardcore Volume 1, 1974-1977' (Essential ESSCD 134)

The Dickies

THE DICKIES

This band, from California, were the clown princes of punk's early years. With Leonard Graves Phillips on vocals, Stan Lee guitar, Chuck Wagon on keyboards, bass player Billy Club (bass) and Karlos Kaballero on drums, they operated at just the one speed – maniacally fast. Having presumably heard what The Ramones were doing on the other side of the country, The Dickies entered the same basic race for the end of the song, but added their own key ingredient – they would cover songs already familiar through more sedate treatments, and go for the novelty sell. The initial comic trot through Black Sabbath's 'Paranoid' didn't seem too outrageous, but when the band progressed to 'Eve Of Destruction', the Christmas carol 'Silent Night' and – most hilariously of all – the Moody Blues' 'Nights In White Satin', the joke became their raison d'etre. Perhaps tellingly, despite the band's US origins, and their signing to a normally laid-back mainstream L.A. label, A&M, all their commercial success came in Britain, where they had six consecutive hits between 1978 and 1980, with the deliberately potty 'Banana Splits (The Tra La La Song)' making the Top 10. They also had two chart albums in the UK in 1979, of which 'The Incredible Shrinking Dickies' was a Top 20 success. By the end of 1980, the joke had finally worn out its welcome, and The Dickies vanished into oblivion (and some solo work), but it was fun having them as punk's equivalent of the Bonzo Dog Doo-Dah Band while they lasted.

DISCHARGE

Led by angry young vocalist Cal (Kevin) Morris and bass player Rainy, who were to be the long-term core of a very flexible band, Discharge were in the vanguard of the new wave of aggressively angry working-class punk which surfaced in Britain diring the first three years of the 1980s. Hailing from Stoke-On-Trent in the West Midlands potteries country, they were the first signing to an appropriately-named local indie label, Clay Records, which was run by London escapee Mike Stone, a former employee of Beggars Banquet who had been involved in the career of first-wave punkers The Lurkers.

Visually sporting the mohicans, leathers, bovver boots and the other trappings of what became the general, overtly intimidatory image of early-80s punk, the band's musical trademarks were speed, aggression and much deliverate noise overkill, which provided an apt backdrop to their machine-gun lyrical rants against their most disliked aspects of British life – which actually encompassed most aspects, from unemployment and urban youth deprivation to warfare and the military. The latter, especially – despite their ever-aggressive stance, Discharge were, in a traditional sense, pacifists, and their material steadily became stridently more anti-war through their early career.

Their records, despite humble origins, were successful from the outset, the 1980 debut EP 'Realities Of War' eventually selling upwards of 30,000 copies after constant re-pressings to cater for a continuing demand. It made the indie chart, and opened the way for a successful string of follow-up singles and EPs, of which 'Why', in May 1981, topped the indie chart for two weeks, and 'Never Again', later in the same year, crossed over to the mainstream chart to surface at No.64. The band became a major UK touring attraction in 1981 and '82, co-headlining the Apocalypse Now punk package with Anti-Pasti, The Exploited and others, and their appeal by the Spring of 1982 was such that their anti-war album 'Hear Nothing, See Nothing, Say Nothing' made No.40 on the national LP

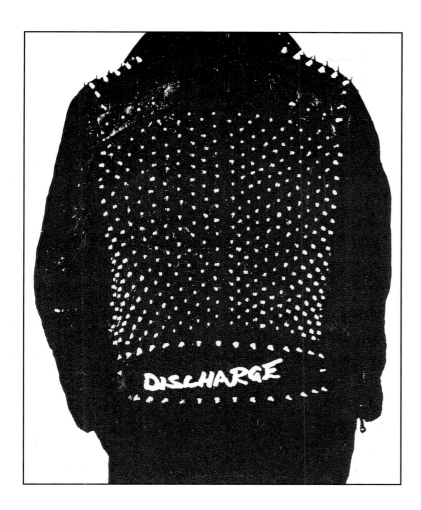

chart, and remained in the best sellers for a month.

So closely tied were Discharge into the style and substance of the early 80s angry wave of punk (despite a constantly fluctuating personnel), it was probably inevitable that their commercial fortunes would ebb away with that movement, which had retreated to rock's sidelines once again by the middle of the decade. The band recorded further albums, notably 'Never Again' and 'Grave New World' in 1984 and 1986 respectively, and reworked their style into what would probably now be termed thrash metal in an effort to progess past their punk roots, but while this undoubtedly gathered some new fans, it lost them a far larger share of the original punk following, which they have never regained to anything like the same degree despite continuing as a performing unit into the 1990s. The legacy of the early style has probably survived better than the band themselves, with its rapid-fire aggression that has been an acknowledged influence on overdrive metallurgists such as Metallica.

DISORDER

Like Chaos UK, Disorder were a protest-motivated punk quartet from Bristol, formed in 1980. Unlike the aforementioned band, they tried but failed to get themselves signed to Bristol's own Riot City punk label after Vice Squad, on whose behalf the label hads been formed, vetoed the idea. In response Disorder (initially Dean on vocals, Steve on guitar, Mick on bass and Virus on drums) simply formed their own label, imaginitively named Disorder, and managed to get this marketed via Riot City. A series of EPs – 'Complete Disorder', 'Distortion To Deafness' and 'Material Obsession' — followed, featuring tracks like 'Violent Crime, Provocated War and Bullshit

Everyone'. The band also made several albums between 1980 and 1985, including 'Perdition', 'Under The Scalpel Blade' and 'Live In Oslo'.

The band's line-up, however, proved less stable than the conviction that they apparently displayed in their material. Bass player Mick left after the first EP, to be replaced first of all by Steve Robinson, the boyfriend of Vice Squad's Beki Bondage, and then by Taff, formerly with The X-Certs Review. Vocalist Dean also fled the nest a couple of releases down the line, and the band's roadie – called Boobs, and male, despite the name – was talked into filling the vacancy in time for the 'Perdition' album. Finally, Virus left after a number of comically tragic European tour experiences, and someone named Glenn took over behind the drum kit for the remainder of the band's recording career.

Recommended CD listening:'Complete Disorder' (Anagram CDPUNK 46)

THE DRONES

One of the earliest punk bands to form in Manchester, in the latter part of 1976, the Drones were a quartet comprising M.J. Drone on vocals and guitar, Gus Callender on lead guitar, Steve Cundell on bass and Pete Howells on drums. Playing on a scene which included The Buzzcocks, Slaughter & The Dogs and Warsaw (who would mutate into Joy Division), they were to fall by the wayside far faster than these contemporaries, probably due to an unwillingness (or inability) to move on from the strictures of a punk syle blueprinted by The Pistols, yet in the earliest days of the genre they were arguably the leaders of the local scene, becoming an early attraction at Manchester's Electric Circus club, and one of the first acts from the Manchester scene to migrate down to London to play on a regular basis at the Roxy. They made a clutch of records during 1977 and '78 beginning with the EP 'Temptations Of A White Collar Worker' on the tiny Ohms label, then moving to the hardly higher-profile Valer Records for 'Bone Idol' and, at the end of 1977, an album titled 'Further Temptations'. All sold minimally, and the album in particular became almost impossible to find in its original form. The majority of record buyers only heard the band via their song 'Persecution Complex', which was included on Virgin's 'Short Circuit' – Live At The Electric Circus' compilation. By the middle of 1978, The Drones had disbanded.

Recommended CD listening: 'Further Temptations' (augmented with 7 bonus tracks taken from singles) (Anagram CD PUNK 20)

Above and opposite, Ian Dury

IAN DURY

When the late-70s punk explosion came in Britain, Ian Dury was one of those performers who in theory should have been swept out of contention by the new broom of spiky-haired rockers, since he was a comparative old-timer; a veteran of the pub-rock scene via the gigging favourites (and record no-hopers) Kilburn & The High Roads. The fact that he instead rode the new wave to major commercial success was due to the fact that Dury, like Elvis Costello, found himself acceptable to a punk-orientated audience without too much change of style from the jazzy funk with gently incisive lyrics that he'd always played. His use of the working class idiom also helped his street cred, while (again like Costello) he served as something of a role model – as much subconsciously as anything – to the more creative songwriting minds of the punk genre, whose ultimate musical aspirations went further than three chords and an on-stage rant. In the meantime, the younger bands were happy to share that stage with Dury.

Dury's most influential work was probably his first as a soloist – both the single 'Sex & Drugs & Rock & Roll' and the album 'New Boots And Panties', both recorded for Stiff in the latter half of 1977. Oddly, the single failed to chart while the album went on to be a consistent seller for most of the next year. In their wake, Dury and his long-time writing partner Chaz Jankel formed the Blockheads, who then backed Dury on a string of singles which did succeed – 'What A Waste', 'Reasons To Be Cheerful', and the chart-topping 'Hit Me With Your Rhythm Stick'. The latter two saw singer and band flirting with dance rhythms, though when punk's commercial clout began to give way in 1980-81 to the New Romantic and jazz-funk dance scenes, Dury's chart star, significantly, faded rapidly alongside it, his restrained brand of revolutionary music apparently needing the ragged energy of the new wave scene in which to find its clearest focus.

Recommended CD listening: 'Sex And Drugs And Rock And Roll' (Demon FIENDCD 69)

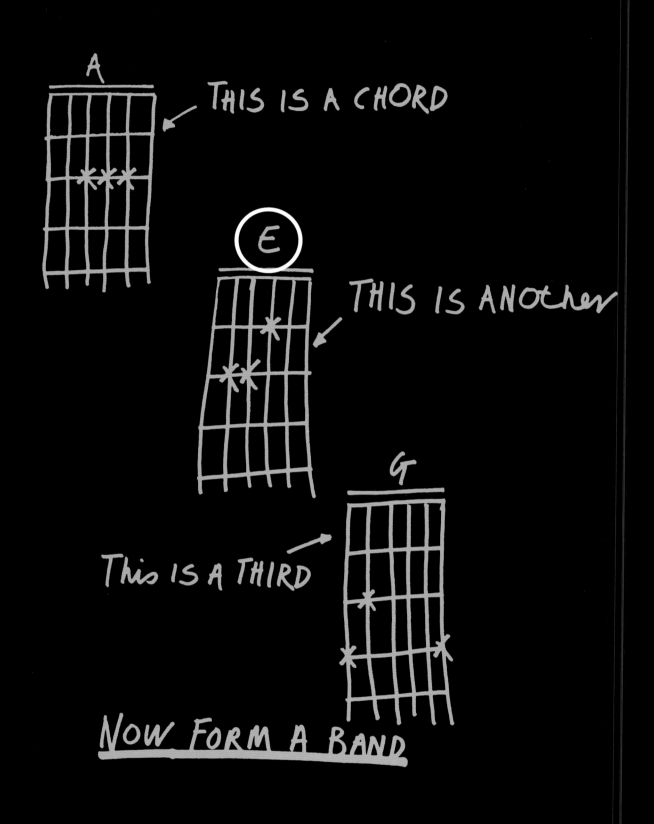

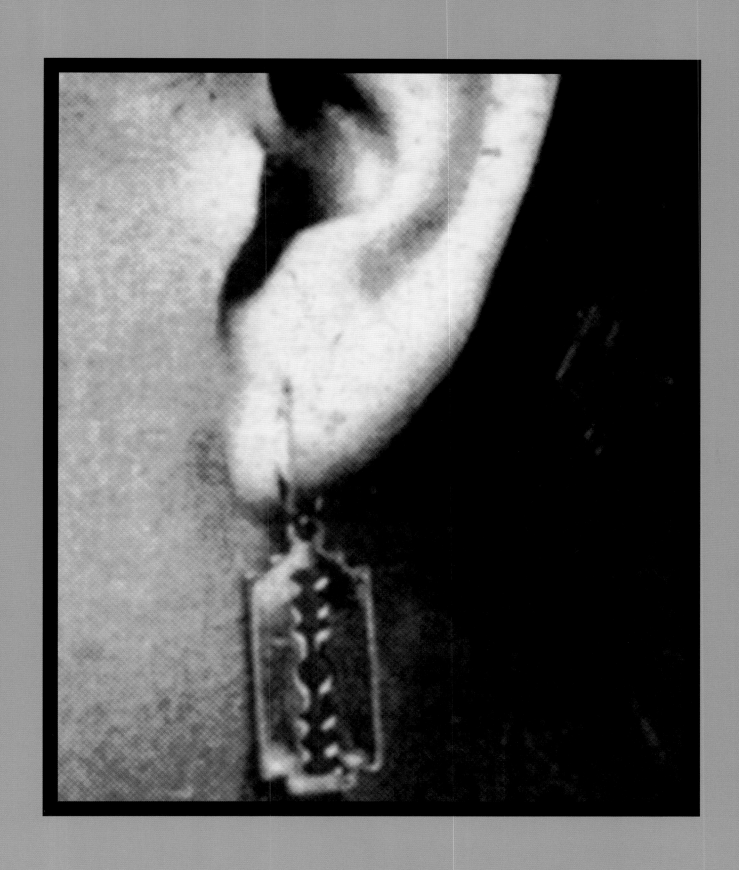

Barrie Masters, fronting Eddie and The Hot Rods

EATER

Eater's main claim to fame on the crowded British punk scene was that they were younger than anybody else playing on that scene. When the group formed during 1976, naming themselves from a line in an old Marc Bolan song, all four members were still at school. Vocalist and songwriter Andy Blade, guitarist Brian Chevette and bassist Ian Woodcock were all 15 years old, while their drummer, who was introduced to them by Rat Scabies of The Damned, and adopted the potentially ominous name of Dee Generate, was a mere 14.

Eater built a rapid repertoire, by their own admission, by tacking on their own lyrics to variations on old Velvet Underground numbers (and were also to cover Lou Reed's 'Sweet Jane' and 'Waiting For The Man'). After launching their live career with a gig in Manchester in November 1976 (at which The Buzzcocks supported them), then being recorded by EMI as part of the Harvest 'Live At The Roxy' album, the quartet – in true punk fashion, still getting to grips with playing their instruments – were signed by The Label, one of the rash of new London indie labels 'Outside View' was their first release, in March 1977, and several singles, an album and a 12-inch live EP (titled 'Get Your Yo-Yos Out', in an oblique reference to The Stones) followed. None of the records, however, charted, since Eater rarely got

any airplay, and early music press fascination with their extreme youth and regulation bad behaviour soon developed into throwaway put-downs, which painted an admittedly fairly ordinary band as nothing more than mere gimmick merchants.

After Eater eventually split at the end of the 1970s, Blade pursued a low-key solo career, with no greater success. Dee Generate, meanwhile, eventually cast aside both his nom-de-punk and yobbish image, to become a social worker!

Recommended CD listening: 'The Compleat Eater' (Anagram CD PUNK 10)

EDDIE AND THE HOT RODS

Formed in the mid-1970s in South-East Essex, Eddie & The Hot Rods were, initially, a high-energy R&B band much in the vein of their close neighbours and friendly rivals Dr. Feelgood, who, by this time, were already a major concert draw and top album–selling act. However, as they hit the London live circuit, The Hot Rods' more youthful profile, compounded by the punky stage persona of lead singer Barrie Masters, saw them being lumped (by the music press, at least) with the rising ranks of punkdom. Signed by

Island at the beginning of 1976, the band (whose other original members were guitarist Dave Higgs, bassist Paul Gray, drummer Steve Nicol and harmonica player Lew Lewis, plus a stage dummy named Eddie who accounted for half of their name) missed the chart with their first two releases (including a zippy revival of Sam The Sham's 'Wooly Bully'), but reached the Top 50 with the third, an EP recorded live at London's Marquee club which showed them at their high-octane best. The fact that on this disc they played only treasured oldies (? & The Mysterians' '96 Tears', Bob Seger's 'Get Out Of Denver', Them's 'Gloria' and The Stones' 'Satisfaction') still seemed lost on those who would lump The Hot Rods with the three-chord nihilists who played the same club circuit. Harp blower Lewis, an R&B man to the core, departed after the first single, possibly alienated by having to live up to this false perception.

The band, with ranks boosted by former Kursaal Flyers guitarist Graham Douglas, reached their commercial peak during 1977, when 'I Might Be Lying' and 'Do Anything You Wanna Do' both charted strongly, particularly the latter (billing them simply as 'The Rods'), which was a Top 10 hit. Both were driving, high-energy rockers, not owing much to either pub-rock R&B or any prevailing punk style, but seeming to assure The Hot Rods of a rosy commercial future. It was not, however, to happen. The band's record sales evaporated rapidly over the following 18 months: as punk energy gave way to new wave cool, The Hot Rods' cranked-up approach seemed out of step. As members grew restless and moved on (with Paul Gray defecting to The Damned), Barrie Masters was eventually left fronting a skelton crew of newcomers, with disbandment the inevitable consequence following 1981's flop 'Fish 'n' Chips' album. Masters has pulled together several short-lived revivals of the Hot Rods, both on stage and record, in subsequent years.

Recommended CD Listening: 'The End Of The Beginning (The Best Of)' (Island IMCD 156)

A leather-and-high-heels Wayne County

ELECTRIC CHAIRS

Although UK-based and featuring mostly British players, The Electric Chairs were assembled (early in 1977) and fronted by an American, Wayne County. A 10-year veteran of the US alternative scene, having appeared in both New York and London in Andy Warhol's controversial stage production *Pork*, and led the theatre–rock band Queen Elizabeth, County was basically your standard exhibitionist transvestite wierdo with a taste for the bizarre and a talent for aggressive rock music, all of which set him up for a role in the burgeoning British punk scene. Originally named the Backstreet Boys, the Electric Chairs consisted of County on vocals and stage theatrics, US guitarist Greg Van Cook, and Britishers Val Haller (bass) and J.J. Johnson (drums). Their first single 'Stuck On You', released by Illegal Records in mid-1977, passed with scant notice, but the second, 'Fuck Off', inevitably brought them instant notoriety, drawing not only a total airplay ban, but also the refusal of Pye, the distributor of their new label Safari Records, to handle the single – it had to finally be pressed on a buckshee indie label and put into the record shops via the London disc wholesaler Lightning.

The Electric Chairs toured the UK frequently between 1977 and 1979, though in recognition of the group's larger-than-life frontperson, the billing expanded to Wayne County & The Electric Chairs quite early on. The group itself had a couple of personnel changes, firstly when Henri Padovani, previously with The Police, came in as second guitarist, and then when original axeman Greg Van Cook left early in 1978, to be replaced

by fellow American Eliot Michaels. Throughout this period, they recorded profusely for Safari, cutting three albums and a string of singles, and although none of their records charted nationally, several of them sold well beyond the level of most indie releases, notably the single 'Eddie And Sheena' (a strange tale of greaser marrying punk and producing hybrid son) and the EP 'Blatantly Offenzive', which lived up to its title by including not only 'Fuck Off', but also 'Mean Motherfuckin' Man' and 'Toilet Love' (a paen to a New York humiliation club).

The saga finally ground to a halt in the summer of 1979, when County parted from the band and returned to the US – a move prompted by the fact that he was due for a sex-change operation which would complete the transition from man to woman which he had slowly been undertaking with hormones, depilation, cosmetics and clothing for several years. Wayne emerged from it all as Jayne County, in which persona she continued to make music – though with a far lower profile – during the 1980s. The Electric Chairs attempted to continue a County-less recording career during 1980, but the audience interest was nil, and only one single ensued before the group disbanded for good.

Recommended CD listening: 'Rock 'n' Roll Cleopatra' (RPM 119)

ERIC'S

Run by Roger Eagle and Pete Fulwell, among the great unsung hero 'backroom boys' of the UK punk era, Eric's was first a music club, and then an independent record label operated out of the same premises, in Mathew Street, Liverpool (opposite the 1960s site of the Cavern Club, ironically). Both were absolutely essential ingredients in the development of the late-70s punk and new wave movement on Merseyside, providing the major outlet for what developed into a veritable second coming of Liverpool groups in the early 1980s.

The venue opened in October 1976, and was finally closed (by the police) in March 1980. The Sex Pistols were one of the first bands to play a gig there, mere days after the opening, and most of the rest of the punk names followed suit as they began to tour nationally. Perhaps even more importantly, though, local acts began to form from the ranks of people whose first experience of the music live was in the Eric's audience. Merseyside bands who played their first gigs at Eric's included The Teardrop Explodes, Echo & The Bunnymen (both on the same day – Nov 15th, 1977), Wah! Heat, Orchestral Manoeuvres In The Dark, The Yachts, the short-lived Mystery Girls (Julian Cope, Pete Burns, Pete Wylie and Phil Hurst), and Big In Japan, in whose ranks at the time were Holly Johnson, Budgie (later of Siouxsie & The Banshees), David Balfe (Teardrop Explodes) and Bill Drummond (KLF).

Big In Japan also had the first single on the Eric's label ('Big In Japan' in Nov 1977), while later releases came from Holly (Johnson), Pink Military and The Frantic Elevators (with Mick Hucknall). A compilation album, 'The Jukebox At Eric's', anthologised some of the classic rare American punk and rock singles which did indeed get played on the club's jukebox – one assumes inspiring the ardently musical clientele.

ESSENTIAL LOGIC

Laura Logic, at 15 an original member of X-Ray Spex (she played sax, but should have been at school) in the latter's formative days prior to their EMI signing, formed her own band, Essential Logic, early in 1978 after leaving art college. Initially recording for their own Cells label, a co-operative deal with Rough Trade, and later moving to Virgin, this quintet (Logic on lead vocals, with Ashley Buff aka Philip Legg on guitar, Mark Turner on bass, Rich Tea(!) on drums and Dave Wright on second tenor) made four or five singles (including their definitive piece, 'Aerosol Burns') and the album 'Beat Rhythm News' over the next two years; all showcased a deceptively ramshackle sax-driven rhythmic style with Logic playing the punk banshee out front. With very little commercial success, their eventual disintegration was inevitable, but Logic persisted in her musical efforts for long enough to also produce a less way-out 1980 solo album, 'Pedigree Charm', and to guest with the likes of Red Crayola, The Raincoats and The Swell Maps.
Recommended CD listening: 'Pedigree Charm' (Virgin 2345 2)(NB DUMMY)

THE EXPLOITED

From Edinburgh, where they were formed in 1980, The Expoloited were to
become one of the leading names of the renewed wave of punk which
came the fore in the UK in 1981-82 – a ranting, deliberately ugly and
aggressive style closely allied to the Oi! movement. The band were very
much a visual archetype of their moment in punk time, with the intimidating
technicolour mohican hairstyle sported by vocalist Wattie Buchan, and the
complimentary studs-and-leather sartorial leanings of his cohorts, guitarist
Big John, bassist Gary and drummer Dru Sticks. It was a look shared by
scores of neophyte punk outfits spluttering into pissed-off action around the
country as the renewed wave of 1980s punk got into gear.

The Exploited first hit vinyl in October
1980 with an EP on their own Exploited
label, marketed by indie distributor Red
Rhino. Its three tracks – 'Army Life',
'Crashed Out' and 'Fuck The Mods' –
typified the band's lyrical concerns – rants
against authority, unemployment, the
police, the military and just about anybody else who stood still for too long, plus
anthems with chant-along choruses
extolling the virtues of an anarchistic,
get–off–my–back lifestyle. Both this and
the similarly self-released 'Exploited Barmy Army'
follow-up EP made the indie charts, and they were
signed early in 1981 by Secret Records, to see their initial
single for the label, 'Dogs Of War', hit the national chart at
No.63, and their debut album 'Punk's Not Dead' reach both
the No.20 spot nationally and the No.1 position for two
weeks on the indie chart.

A high-profile national tour in 1981 with fellow
ranters Discharge, Anti-Pasti and Chron Gen brought
the band to wider awareness, while their single 'Dead
Cities' shot to No.31 and actually delivered them a
slot on *Top Of The Pops* – an event akin to inviting Attila
The Hun and a few mates to the Queen's garden
party, which nonetheless did The Exploited's
record sales no harm at all, as two more singles
('Attack' and 'Don't Let 'Em Grind You Down',
with Anti-Pasti) and two further albums
('Exploited Live' and 'Troops Of Tomorrow')
also climbed into the charts. The latter LP, in
fact, scored their highest mainstream chart
ranking of No.17, and was on the list for nearly
three months.

Inevitably, the band's commercial bubble burst,
when the spotlight moved away from the punk/Oi!
renewal, and they proved too entrenched in their style
and attitude to change and grow with the times.
Continuing to record throughout the 1980s, latterly on
labels like Pax, Connexion and Dojo (which has also
reissued their early catalogue), the band are active to
this day, with a committed, nostalgic audience still able to
connect to their angry early 80s timewarp.

**Recommended CD listening: 8 tracks on Secret Records: 'The
Punk Singles Collection' (Anagram CDPUNK 13)**

SNIFFIN' GLUE..
+ OTHER ROCK 'N' ROLL HABITS FOR PUNKS! ⓐ

NO.1 OF MANY, WE HOPE!

THIS THING IS NOT MEANT TO BE READ...IT'S FOR SOAKING IN GLUE AND SNIFFIN'.

IN THE FIRST ISSUE:

THE RAMONES

ALBUM & CONCERT REVIEWS!

 PLUS

BLUE OYSTER CULT

RE-REVIEW OF ALL THEIR ALBUMS!

+ PUNK REVIEWS

ALBUMS, SINGLES & CONCERTS!

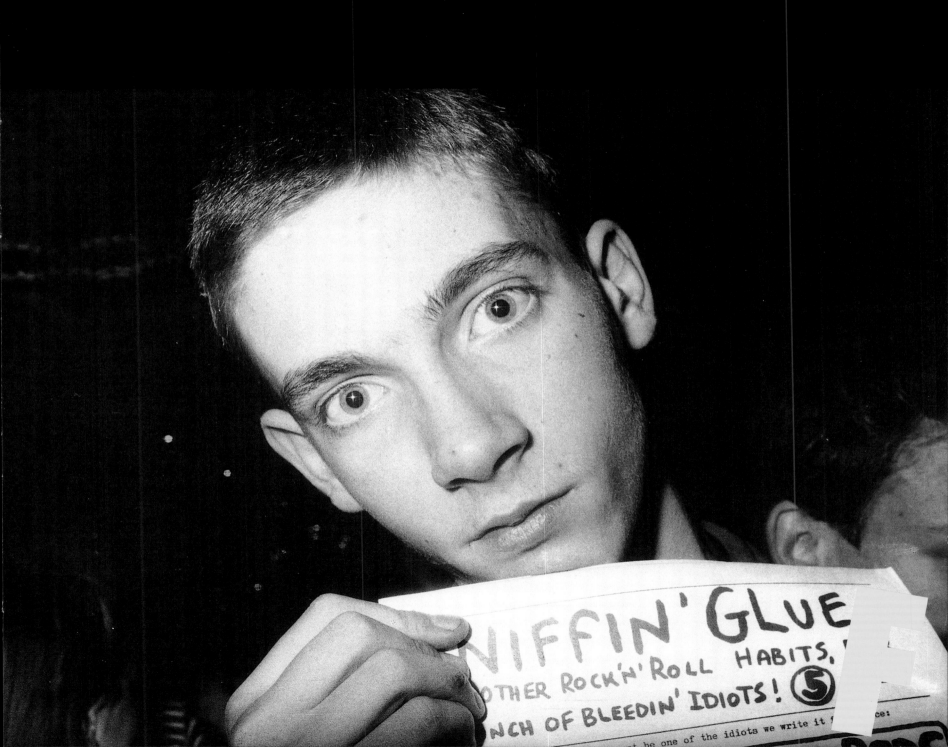

NIFFIN' GLUE
OTHER ROCK'N' ROLL HABITS,
NCH OF BLEEDIN' IDIOTS! ⑤

t be one of the idiots we write it f

THE 4-SKINS

The East End quartet with the calculatedly provocative name (sexual *and* skinhead connotations), who formed in 1979, came to punk prominence as part of the Oi! movement, in the company of Infa-Riot, The Business, and several other London-based outfits with a yobby stance and often genuinely violent fans. They were one of the first of this new wave of bands to capture national music press coverage: lead singer Gary Hodges was pictured on *Sounds'* front cover of November 1, 1980 to illustrate Oi! svengali Garry Bushell's feature on the movement within, and they made their vinyl debut with the tracks 'Chaos' and 'Wonderful World' on the *Sounds*-sponsored 'Oi! - The Album' compilation which was initially sold through mail order via the paper.

Inevitably, considering their high profile, The 4-Skins were always prime targets for those who gravitated to make deliberate trouble at Oi! gigs. No sooner had they cut their first single 'One Law For Them' (released on their own indie label, Clockwork Fun), than the band were involved in the biggest Oi!-related public disturbance of all, a full-scale riot erupted during a gig (featuring The 4-Skins and other bands) at the Hamborough Tavern in Southall, South-West London, in July 1981. An army of police fought punks, the venue was badly damaged by fire, and the band's guitarist Steve was one of many who suffered incidental injuries during the melee.

With the media at their throats, The 4-Skins quit – in the case of singer Gary and guitarist Steve, for good. The others eventually regrouped with new recruits towards the end of the year, and were signed by Secret Records, which released two further singles, 'Yesterday's Heroes' and 'Lowlife', and in April 1982, the album 'The Good, The Bad And The 4-Skins', which managed a creditable No.80 on the national charts. The band also appeared on Secret's 'Bollocks To Christmas' compilation EP in December 1981. Later, they thought twice about releasing a deliberate shift into 2-Tone ska territory under a new name of the Plastic Gangsters, while their final single 'Seems To Me' failed to get issued at all when the Secret label closed down.

Recommended CD listening: 4 tracks on Secret Records: 'The Punk Singles Collection' (Anagram CDPUNK 13)

THE FALL

The Fall were formed in Manchester in January 1977, right on the crest of punk's first wave. Unlike almost every other band of that period, they would still be a high-profile performing unit in the mid-1990s, albeit after a likely world record number of personnel changes. The one constant factor was the band's vocalist, songwriter, general visionary and overall driving force, Mark E. Smith. He had his own unique take on punk's arrogant but blurred nihilism: an uncompromising, take-it-or-leave-it, overtly Northern philosophy which gave a suitably uptight attitude to the band's usually wilfully lateral music and lyrics.

The original Fall line-up, comprising Smith, Martin Bramah (guitar), Una Baines (keyboards), Tony Friel (bass) and Karl Burns (drums) played their first gig in May 1977, and made their first vinyl appearance a year later via two tracks on Virgin's 'Short Circuit: Live At The Electric Circus' Manchester punk compilation. Shortly after, they signed to the indie Step Forward label, and released the three-track 'Bingo Master's Break Out' EP, a non-charting but nonetheless key single (if only for its lyrical strangeness) in the punk canon.

Their sojourn with Step Forward lasted the band through 1979, with three more singles: 'It's The New Thing', 'Rowche Rumble' and 'Fiery Jack' — all quite as offbeat as they sound – plus the studio album 'Dragnet' and the live set 'Live At The Witch Trials'. By now the line-up was already a shifting kaleidoscope, with many of the original band departed, and others like guitarists Marc Riley and Craig Scanlon, bassist Steve Hanley, keyboardist Yvonne Pawcett and drummer Mike Leigh either quasi-permanently or at least passing through.

After the early punk bands had either charted or departed, and the early 80s wave of studded and mohicaned pacifist ranters took up the torch, The Fall merely continued on their eclectic way with never more than a nod to either faction. A 1980 change of label to Rough Trade ensured a continuation of Smith's angular odyssey, manifested in the albums 'Totale's Turns (It's Now Or Never)' and 'Grotesque (After The Gramme)', both of which topped the indie chart in 1980, and were accompanied by the best selling Fall singles yet, 'How I Wrote Elastic Man' and 'Totally Wired'.

As the decade moved on, the musical focus of the band would shift subtly when Smith's American wife Brix, a strong guitarist with a (theoretically incompatible) 60s-hankering melodic sensibility, joined him in the front line. Later, there would be the hit single phase, when mind-boggling covers of R. Dean Taylor's 'There'a Ghost In My House' and The Kinks' 'Victoria' gave them Top 40 hits. Smith's own later songs like 'Hit The North' and 'Hey! Luciani' found similar chart status, while from 'Hex Enduction Hour' in 1982, The Fall's albums would also begin to hit the mainstream charts, culminating in a top 20 placing for 'The Frenz Experiment' in 1988. Most of this later history falls outside the story of punk, but The Fall's lasting importance as a band who started squarely within the genre and in their own way continued it single handedly for — literally – decades, cannot be underestimated.

Recommended CD listening: 'Totale's Turns (It's Now Or Never)' (Dojo CD 83)

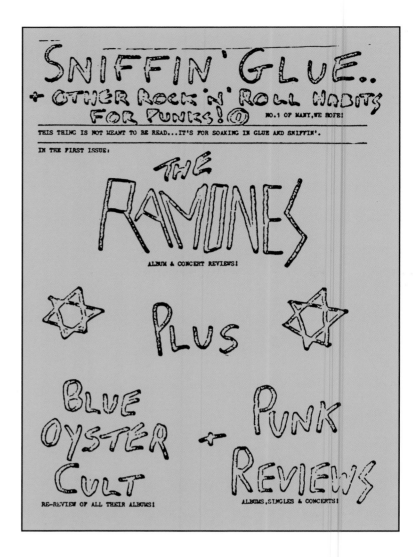

Mark Perry, known more familiarly at the time as Mark P.

FANZINES

Given the do-it-yourself-right-now ethic of early punk, which tended to make it up and make do as it went along, it isn't surprising that, alongside the indigenous fashions and the small labels, an amateur press corps also flourished, using the most basic office methods (inked-roller duplicators and photocopied cut-and-paste) to produce instant magazines by fans for fans, fired by the same energy and anti-establishment ethos as the music itself. Completely non-commercial, these fanzines were generally produced with zero investment and mostly lost money – some were even given away free as a matter of principle. Regardless of this, the key titles soon developed a distinct D.I.Y. graphic style which became part of the overall punk image, and was soon being borrowed wholesale for record ads and sleeves, and even began to infiltrate the mainstream rock press.

By far the best known and most influential British punk fanzine was *Sniffin 'Glue (And Other Rock'n'Roll Habits)*, started by south Londoner Mark Perry in July 1976, ostensibly inspired by NME journalist Nick Kent's review of the first Ramones album. Perry would keep his xeroxed mag going until its priorities were overtaken by those of his band, Alternative TV (by which time he was shifting 10,000 copies), but in the meantime, the competition sprang up in vast profusion in *Sniffin' Glue*'s wake: *Ripped And Torn*, *Out There*, *Buzz*, *Self Abuse*, *No Future*, *Sounds Of The*

Westway, *Situation 3*, *Alternative Ulster*, *Bondage*, *In The City*, *I Wanna Be Your Dog*, *Negative Reaction*, *London's Burning* (a Clash mag), *Strangled* (The Stranglers), and scores more. Within a couple of years there was a similar deluge in America, which had no tradition of weekly music papers, and thus even more of an immediacy gap to fill. *Teenage Rampage*, *Punk Lust*, *Blister*, *Inaudible Noise*, *Public Threat*, *Rag In Chains*, *Sick Transit* and *Smegma Journal* were among the titles which, while the explosion lasted, filled it.

For all their ephemeral nature and rapid disposability, the fanzines were (and have continued to be, though their post-punk successors), ideal proving grounds for people who felt sufficiently moved by music to write about it: a lot of professional rock writers of the 1980s (and quite a number of musicians) made their enthusiastic and inspired start in the fanzines, labouring for nothing but love.

FATAL MICROBES

Short-lived in themselves, The Fatal Microbes produced girl vocalist Honey Bane, who for a while was selected by the media as one of punk's somewhat dubious line of pin-ups, chronologically fitting between Jordan and Vice Squad's Beki Bondage. In the spring of 1979, at the time of The Fatal Microbes' vinyl debut, Honey (real name Donna Boyle) was a 14-year old resident of St. Charles Home for 'difficult' teenagers, and effectively in the care of the social services. The group gained the chance to record via a link with The Poison Girls, an almost wilfully alternative band in the Crass mould, whose lead singer Vi Subversa happened to be the mother of The Microbes' guitarist Pete Fender. Small Wonder Records, in one of its many

PUNK!

one-single deals, released an EP containing The Fatal Microbes' 'Violence Grows' and 'Beautiful Pictures' on one side, and two Poison Girls tracks on the other. When demand continued after the initial pressing had sold out, the two Microbes tracks were then reissued as a Small Wonder single in their own right.

Perhaps inevitably, in view of the fact that the spotlight was firmly fixed on the wayward vocalist, the band lasted no longer than that first record, and Honey Bane immediately struck out as a soloist, recording a three-track EP on the Cross label (with Cross themselves as backing band) which became a sizeable indie chart hit in 1980, and then signing with EMI's Zonophone label to produce two moderately-sized national hit singles in 'Turn Me On, Turn Me Off' and 'Baby Love', both in 1981. After this, she faded from view musically, but had one more moment of notoriety when she featured in an explicit on-stage sex scene with former Skids lead singer Richard Jobson while acting in a London fringe theatre production.

FEAR

A quartet comprising Lee Ving (vocals), Philo Cramer (guitar), Derf Scratch (bass) and Spit Stix (drums), Fear were formed in San Francisco in 1980, and were brief luminaries on the West Coast hardcore punk circuit, alongside the likes of X, Black Flag and The Circle Jerks. Like all those bands, they had several tracks (including 'Fear Anthem' and 'I Love Livin' In The City') on the Slash Records compilation album 'The Decline Of Western Civilisation', and could be seen playing in the documentary film of the same name. The same label also released their own album 'Fear' early in 1982, but its sales were lacklustre, and no follow-up was forthcoming.

PATRIK FITZGERALD

Patrik Fitzgerald was a unique figure in the UK 1970s punk scene, because he played an acoustic guitar (at one point with just five strings), and he wasn't even really a singer, but a poet: an acoustic poet working within the punk idiom.

It might have been otherwise, because early in 1976, North Londoner Fitzgerald was one of the dozens of the proto-punk players who auditioned for Tony James and Mick Jones' never-to-be band, the London SS, getting a firm thumbs-down because he wasn't much good with an electric guitar. He had previously also been rejected, along with his first songs, by David Bowie's former manager Ken Pitt.

In 1977, after working for some months with a theatrical group, Fitzgerald submitted a demo tape to Small Wonder Records, launched by the Walthamstow record shop of the same name where he was a regular buyer of punk singles. Small Wonder offered a deal, and during 1978 released two EPs and a 9-track mini-album ('The Paranoid Ward') of acoustic punk-folk songs, mostly ruminations on punk lifestyle ('Make It Safe', 'Safety Pin Stuck In My Heart') and late-70s living in general ('Buy

Patrik Fitzgerald

Me Sell Me, Backstreet Boys'). Although only steady sellers, these records brought Fitzgerald sufficient notice and rock press coverage to get him on to punk bills at clubs like the Roxy and the Vortex, while he also toured as support act with The Jam, and came to the attention of their record label Polydor, which signed him in October 1978 – although two Polydor singles (one featuring Buzzcocks drummer John Maher) and an album, 'Grubby Stories', all released the following year, meant comparatively little.

Out of the spotlight as his punk connections faded, Fitzgerald continued to write, record and perform, touring widely around Europe's 'alternative' club circuit during the 1980s. Subsequent albums included 'Drifting Towards Violence' on the Himalaya label, and 'Gifts And Telegrams' and 'Tunisian Twist' on Red Flame.

Recommended CD listening: 'The Very Best Of Patrik Fitzgerald: Safety Pin Stuck In My Heart' (Anagram CD PUNK 31)

FRANTIC ELEVATORS

The Frantic Elevators' chief claim to fame will always be that Mick Hucknall, later a world superstar with Simply Red, was originally one of their number, and that in October 1982, just before they ceased to be, they cut the original version of Hucknall's song 'Holding Back The Years', later to be Simply Red's biggest international hit.

The band were formed by Hucknall in Manchester during 1978, with himself on vocals and guitar, plus guitarist Neil Smith, bassist and keyboards player Brian Turner and drummer Kev Williams. Frantic was their nature as well as their name: apart from being legendary hellraisers on stage, most of their records leaned on the ranting energy of mid-70s punk at a time – against the grain of New Wave boundary-widening, and quite the antithesis of Hucknall's later soul/funk leanings. The band cut four singles stretching over a period of as many years, none of which sold beyond their gigging fan base in the North-West. Each release was on a different independent label: 'Voice In The Dark' (1979) was on TJM, 'You Know What You Told Me' (1980) on Eric's, 'Searching For The Only One' (1981) on Crackin' Up, and finally 'Holding Back The Years' (1982) on No Waiting. Following this one, Hucknall indeed didn't wait any longer, but disbanded The Elevators early in 1983 and marched on to chart glory with what were obviously his true musical aspirations.

FUCK THE SYSTEM
ALL GOVERMENT IS OPPRESSION
KEPT IN LINE WITH
TRUNCHEONS. RIFLE BUTTS
THIS IS STATE CONTROL
HELLO
YERRR
ANTI-SECT
PUS
JAMES
IS
WANKER
BY ROXY
ROXY IS
PREGNANT!
FIDDLE STICKS

PUNK!

Generation X

G.B.H.

The three letters of their name are the traditional police acronym of Grievous Bodily Harm, and the members of this 1980-formed quartet – Colin (vocals), Jock (guitar), Ross (bass) and Wilf (drums) (they never used surnames) – were always happy to let these connotations ride as part of their nihilistic, yobbish image. In fact, the band was originally known, even more directly, as Charged GBH. Accepted legend has it that they played their very first gig on the same day as the 1980 Cup Final, at a benefit event for prostitutes.

After Discharge, with whose aggressive bollocks-to-the-lot-of-you style their music had a lot in common, GBH were the next successful signing to Stoke-on-Trent's lively punk-orientated indie label, Clay Records. Their debut release, during 1981, was the 12-inch EP 'Leather, Bristles, Studs And Acne', which, aside from being a fair description of the boots-and-mohican quartet themselves, contained several tracks which communicated the main gist of the band's lyrical concerns: 'Necrophilia', 'D.O.A.', 'State Executioner' and 'Lycanthropy'. The EP made the indie chart, but its success was bettered (after G.B.H. had supported The Damned, the UK Subs and several other top names at the 'Christmas On Earth' punk spectacular at the Queens Hall, Leeds, in December 1981) during 1982 by the singles 'No Survivors' and 'Give Me Fire', both of which reached the mid-60s on the national singles chart. A bigger seller still was their August 1982 debut album on Clay, 'City Baby Attacked By Rats', which made the No.17 spot nationally and was charted for six weeks. Tracks like 'Slut', 'Big Women' and 'Slit Your Own Throat' were among the tracks so widely devoured by the mainstream audience.

For a band firmly locked into an image and musical stance particular to a couple of years at the beginning of the 1980s, G.B.H. held on to their core audience sufficiently well to keep going for the rest of the decade, though without repeating their early rush of commercial success, and always at the risk of seeming like a parody of their own extreme outlook. Later albums on Clay and later Rough Justice included 'City Babies' Revenge', 'Midnight Madness And Beyond', and 'A Fridge Too Far'.

Recommended CD listening: 'The Clay Years 81-84' (Clay CLAYCD 21)

GENERATION X

In November '76, Tony James (bass and vocals), Billy (guitar) and John Towe (drums) had played just a handful of disastrous gigs as Chelsea with Gene October (who wasn't willing to sing any Idol/James material), when they decided to quit en masse rather than oust October. Deciding upon the name Generation X (from the title of a book on 60s youth culture spotted on Idol's mother's shelves), they recruited Bob Andrews (guitar) from his youth club band Paradox, and only three weeks after the Chelsea split were rehearsed and playing their first gig with Idol as lead vocalist at London's Central College Of Art & Design. Just before Christmas, they also played the opening night of Covent Garden's Roxy Club.

Towe left in May 1977 (to re-emerge in Alternative TV and later the Adverts), and was replaced by former Subway Sect drummer Mark Laff shortly before the band's first UK tour, which was observed by several rival A&R men. Signed by Chrysalis in the Summer, they made the UK chart with their first single, the anthemic 'Your Generation', in September, reaching No.36. The follow-up 'Wild Youth' hiccoughed, but the 60s tribute 'Ready Steady Go' (a distinctly power-pop, rather than punk, excursion) was a hit early in 1978, and their eponymous first album reached the Top 30 in its wake. Idol in particular became one of punk's recognisable celebrities, with his bleach-blonde spiky hair and permanent sneer, and the persona would prove durable, sustaining him equally well through his later highly successful international solo career.

1979 was Generation X's most commercially successful year, with 'King Rocker' brushing the Top 10, and 'Valley Of The Dolls', 'Friday's Angels' and the Ian Hunter-produced album 'Valley Of The Dolls' also charting. During 1980, they officially shortened their name to Gen X (as most people referred to them anyway), and continued to tour busily – visiting Japan among other places – but differing views about future musical directions were now affecting the band's previous unity, and in November both Laff and Andrews departed, to be replaced by former Clash drummer Terry Chimes and ex-Chelsea guitarist James Stephenson. This line-up recorded the final Gen X album 'Kiss Me Deadly', which was released in January 1981, but it sold poorly and failed to chart. This was enough for Idol, who quit immediately and left for New York, where he linked up with Keith Forsey (who had produced the last LP) and started planning his solo career, for which he would remain based in America. The band, inevitably, broke up in the wake of his departure. Co-founder James would spend some time out of the spotlight before rebounding in 1986 with the short-lived pose-rock outfit Sigue Sigue Sputnik.

Recommended CD listening: 'Generation X' (Chrysalis CCD 1169)

GIRLS AT OUR BEST

Even at their best, they weren't all girls. A quartet formed in Leeds early in 1980 by former members of The Butterflies and The Expelaires, the band consisted of Jo (Judy Evans) on vocals, Jez (James Alan) on guitar, Terry (Gerard Swift) on bass, and Titch (Carl Harper) on drums. Never pure punks in a musical sense, their material combined some of the straight ahead urgency of the basic genre with a quirky alternative rock blend. Their debut single, coupling 'Warm Girls' and the equally well-rated 'Getting Nowhere Fast', was the first release on the imaginatively-named Record label, in April 1980. Distributed by Rough Trade, it sold well enough to warrant a follow-up, 'Politics', six months later, on a joint Rough Trade/Record label. These releases, and their name, gave them something of a radical feminist image (akin to that of The Au Pairs), which was almost certainly deliberate, but ironic in the context of a mixed-sex band with only the singer actually a girl.

Two more singles, 'Go For Gold' and 'Fast Boyfriends', appeared on the Happy Birthday label in 1981, selling less well than the earlier releases, and possibly prompting the departure of both Terry and Titch during 1982. Following that year's 'Heaven', on yet another indie label, God, the band faded from view.

THE HEARTBREAKERS

The Heartbreakers resulted from coincidental fragmentation in two other New York bands when, almost simultaneously in May 1975, bassist Richard Hell left Television, and guitarist Johnny Thunders and drummer Jerry Nolan parted from The New York Dolls. They immediately united, and within weeks were joined by guitarist Walter Lure. This quartet descended on the New York club circuit, gaining a mixed reputation as no-nonsense rockers but also as unreliable trouble-makers – a combination which kept both a record deal and more lucrative work at arm's length. Nevertheless, they stuck with their cult status for over a year, until in July 1976 Hell jumped ship to form The Voidoids. The other three brought in Billy Rath to replace him, and then, somewhat disillusioned by their declining status in New York, decided to try to make it in Britain.

At the end of 1976, the Heartbreakers supported the Sex Pistols on such dates as survived on the ill-fated 'Anarchy' tour, and then in March the following year signed a record deal with Track, resulting in the single 'Chinese Rocks', which they were still attempting to promote when, in July 1977, they were deported back to the US because their work permits had expired. By September they had returned, but a month later, just as their debut album 'L.A.M.F.' (or 'Like A Mother Fucker') was hitting the shops, Nolan decided to quit, partly over dissatisfaction with the LP's production (by Speedy Keen, ex-Thunderclap Newman). He was persuaded to stay to fulfil live commitments, and played through most of the subsequent UK tour (which helped 'L.A.M.F.' to No.55 in the chart), before finally going back to New York at the end of November. Rath and Lure followed him, and with Thunders electing to stay on in London, the Heartbreakers were, in effect, no more.

After much gigging and recording a solo album, 'So Alone', in the UK, Thunders made a temporary reunion with The Heartbreakers in New York towards the end of 1978 – the blueprint for several such liaisons which would occur during the 1980s, producing a couple of fairly chaotic live albums. Despite an ever more debilitating drink and drugs habit, Thunders would also play and record quite prolifically in his own right through the 80s, and in 1990 he formed a new band, Gang War, with former MC5 member Wayne Kramer. All this was finally stilled, though, when he was found mysteriously dead in a New Orleans hotel room in 1991, probably as the result of a heroin overdose.

Recommended CD listening: 'L.A.M.F. Revisited'(Jungle FREUDCD 04)

RICHARD HELL

Real name Richard Myers, Hell was a seminal figure in punk on both sides of the Atlantic, as much as anything because he gave it much of its early visual image – his wasted appearance, ripped clothes and manic demeanour were all style factors appropriated by Malcolm McLaren on behalf of The Sex Pistols.

From Kentucky, Hell was in New York in 1971 when he met Tom Verlaine and Billy Ficca, and they formed the Neon Boys, a band which got no further than the rehearsal and demo stage. In 1974 they tried again as Television, augmented by Richard Lloyd, and built a New York audience through regular gigs at CBGB's club, but after 12 months Hell left, citing the usual personal and musical differences. Within weeks, he had linked up with Johnny Thunders and Jerry Nolan, who had just departed the New York Dolls for similar reasons, and with guitarist Walter Lure, they formed The Heartbreakers. This band specialised in a sonic blitzkreig act and a similarly over-the-top lifestyle off stage, and struggled to record or tour because of their uncompromising attitude, but Hell still eventually found himself at odds with the others, and split in the summer of 1976, to re-emerge at the end of the year as Richard Hell & the Voidoids, alongside guitarists Robert Quine and Ivan Julian, and drummer Mark Bell.

Having impressed Stiff label founder Jake Riviera when he was in the Heartbreakers, Hell was given a one-off Stiff deal which produced the EP 'Blank Generation', and critical interest in this (despite low sales) led to a deal with Sire and a subsequent album, also titled 'Blank Generation'. The title song became something of a rallying cry for punk itself, even though Hell never managed to turn it (or anything else) into a hit single.

The Voidoids lost drummer Bell to The Ramones during 1978 (he was replaced by Frank Mauro), but the band played successful British tours with The Clash and Elvis Costello, and (again via Jake Riviera) signed another record deal, with the UK Radar label, producing the single 'The Kid With The Replaceable Head'.

Lack of commercial success, and the waning of the original punk wave which he helped inspire, steadily lowered Hell's profile as the 70s ended. The Voidoids regrouped with different personnel several times but recorded infrequently, cutting the further albums 'R.I.P.' (for Reach Out in 1985) and 'Destiny Street' (for I.D. in 1988). Hell himself turned more frequently to stage acting, mostly notably in Susan Seidelman's 'blank generation' drama *Smithereens* in 1982.

Recommended CD listening: 'Blank Generation' (WEA 759926137-2)

P_{UNK!}

Richard Hell

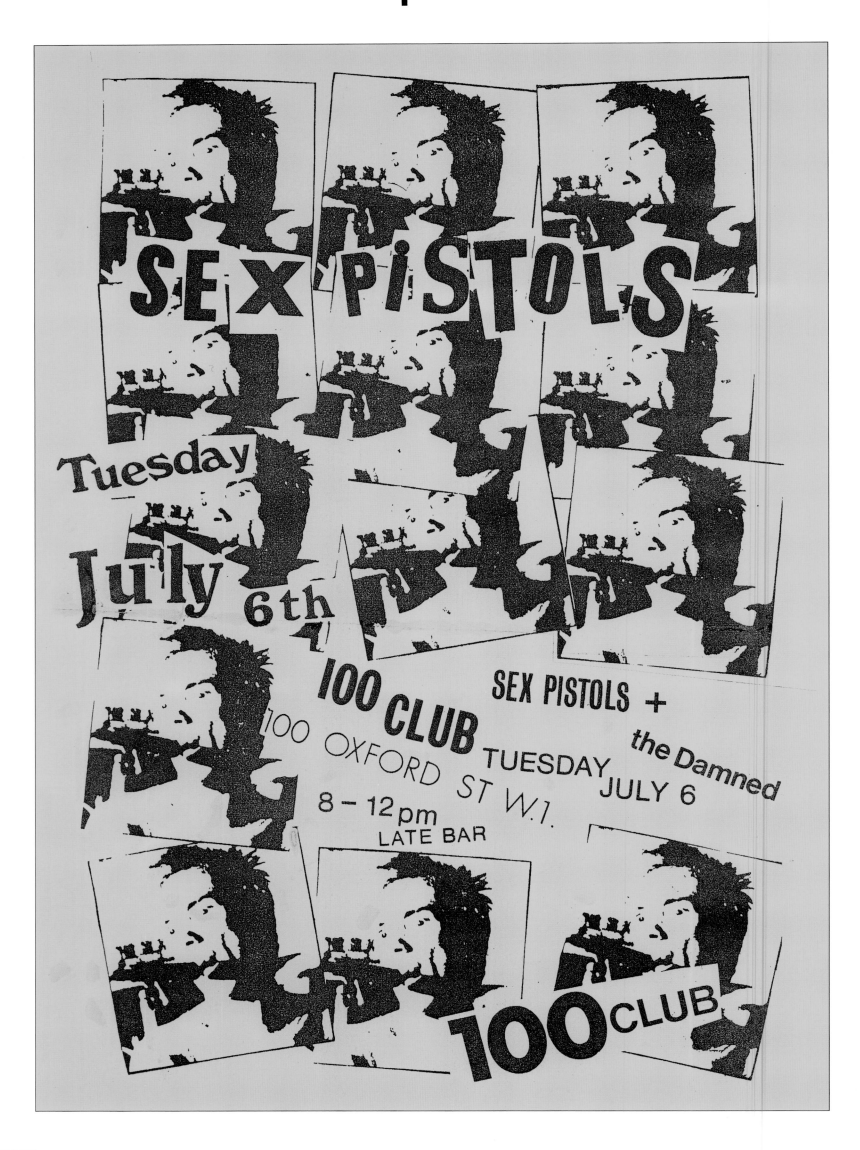

PUNK!

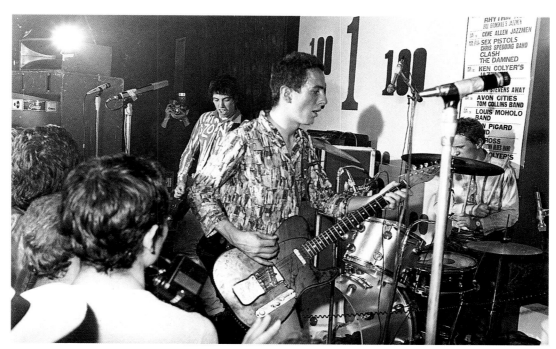

The Pistols (top) and The Clash at the 100 Club Festival

100 CLUB PUNK ROCK FESTIVAL

The 100 Club, a long-established live rock and jazz venue in Oxford Street, in the heart of London's West End, was the site of the first major mass UK exposure of punk to the public – and the music press and record companies – at large. Almost every band which had started to make its name on the punk club circuit over the previous few months took part in the two-night festival, while others played here for the first time, and some musicians even met, prior to forming bands, while hanging out at the now almost legendary event.

The festival took place on Monday 20th and Tuesday 21st September, 1976, about 10 months after the first Sex Pistols gig, and two months after the Mont De Marsan Punk Rock Festival in France. The Monday evening bill featured Vic Goddard & The Subway Sect playing their first gig, the similar debut of a proto-version of Siouxsie & The Banshees (Siouxsie,

Marco Pirroni on guitar, Steve Havoc on bass and Sid Vicious on drums), The Clash (their fourth gig), and bill-toppers The Sex Pistols, who played a lengthy 75-minute set incorporating just about their entire repertoire. The second night included the French band Stinky Toys, The Damned, The Vibrators (with Chris Spedding guesting), and The Buzzcocks. A glass-throwing incident during The Damned's act caused serious injuries to at least one audience member, who was taken to hospital. The police moved in and arrests were made, but they did not attempt to stop the music, since the audience was, if anything, shocked and therefore subdued by the incident. The club management was not impressed, however, and eager to keep its reputation intact, banned punk acts from performing shortly afterwards. By this time, new venues like the Roxy and the Vortex were opening though, and continued exposure of the music was assured.

IJK

IG
GY
PO
P

I'M
BORED.

IGGY & THE STOOGES

Of the several influences which invested the early punk bands with their
snotty aggression and their wired-up, high-speed approach, Iggy Pop and
The Stooges, along with The New York Dolls, were recognisably the closest
antecedents – and often quoted as such by the first-movers on the London
scene. This was despite (or perhaps because of) the fact that The Stooges
had little commercial success and an unsatisfactory, turmoil-ridden history.
Their vocalist Iggy Pop (real name James Osterburg) is often named the
'Godfather of punk', and his on-stage antics, which involved abandoned
manic aggression and occasional self-mutilation, were grist for many a
punk frontman's repertoire of bad behaviour.

The Psychedelic Stooges, as they were originally named, were formed
in Detroit in 1967 by Iggy (who gained his name from drumming with The
Iguanas in 1964) and Ron Asheton, formerly of The Chosen Few. Iggy was
initially the guitarist and Asheton the bassist, but as the line-up coalesced,
Ron took over on guitar and Ig became vocalist and general stage wild
man. The new bassist was Dave Alexander, while Asheton's brother Scott
played drums. A year later, with the adjective gone from their name, they
signed to Elektra, and with ex-Velvet John Cale producing, recorded an
eponymously-titled debut album, released during 1969. It was a small hit,
reaching No. 106 in the American chart, but the 1970 follow-up
'Funhouse' failed to get even that far.

Prior to and following the second album, The Stooges' line-up lost its
stability, as Dave Alexander left (replaced on bass by Zeke Zettner), Bill
Cheatham came and went on second guitar, Steven McKay joined on sax,
and guitarist James Williamson proved a more durable replacement for
Cheatham. However, with Iggy fighting a serious drug habit, the band
became forcibly inactive and in August 1971 the players eventually went
their separate ways.

After meeting David Bowie in 1972 and signing to his management
company, Iggy reformed the band (with both Ashetons and James
Williamson) and got a new deal with Columbia Records, resulting in the
album 'Raw Power', released under the name Iggy & The Stooges. A minor
US success (it reached No.182), this proved, two years or so later, to be
an influence on aspiring punk-orientated musicians which belied its quite
modest sales, thanks to tracks like 'Search And Destroy', 'Penetration',
'Death Trip' and 'Raw Power' itself. Such adulation-to-come did little good
for The Stooges at the time, however, and with sessions for the next album
(eventually released as 'Kill City' in 1978) incomplete, and Iggy himself
burdened by drug and mental problems, the band unravelled for the last
time in January 1974, their legend as punk pioneers secure.

Iggy Pop himself would survive, probably against the odds, to have a
long and intermittently successful solo career, both in music and acting,
stretching into the '90s.

Recommended CD listening: 'Raw Power' (Essential ESSCD 005)

INFA-RIOT

Formed in 1979 as part of the UK punk resurgence alongside bands like
The Cockney Rejects and The 4-Skins, this North London quartet became,
like those contemporaries, tarred with the yobbish Oi! movement tag, and
frequently suffered factional violence at their gigs. They cut their first single
'Five Minute Fashions' in 1980, only to see it languish unissued, but after
topping the bill of the first 'New Punk Convention' concert promoted by
Sounds writer-cum-Oi! champion Garry Bushell, in Southgate (it was cut
short by fighting only 10 minutes into their act), they placed two tracks –
'We Outnumber You' and the appropriate 'Riot Riot' – on the *Sounds* 1981
compilation album 'Strength Through Oi!', which was actually put together
by Bushell.

Towards the end of 1981, Infa-Riot were signed to the Secret label,
where they released two singles, 'Kids Of The 80s' and 'School's Out', and
also joined The Exploited and Chron Gen on the EP 'Britannia Waives The
Rules'. Their biggest seller, however, was their Secret album 'Still Out Of
Order', which hit No.42 in the charts during the Summer of 1982.

**Recommended CD listening: 3 tracks on Secret Records: 'The Punk Singles
Collection' (Anagram CDPUNK 13)**

One of the first punk era's most individual and commercially successful groups originated in 'the jam' which vocalist/guitarist Paul Weller and drummer Rick Buckler would regularly hold during school lunch breaks with several other classmates in Woking, Surrey, during 1973-4. These jammers eventually left school in a regular four-man line-up comprising Weller, Buckler, bassist Bruce Foxton and second guitarist Steve Brookes, though the latter dropped out soon after they began to develop out of local youth club gigging and into the London/South-East club circuit. The remaining trio were influenced to some extent by the burgeoning live punk movement, partly because its audiences were attuned to the high-energy, fast-paced rock in which The Jam were also specialising, but the band's actual focus was taken from two 1960s influences – the early Who (Weller's personal faves), and the English mod sound circa 1966, which was represented visually in The Jam's sharp stage suits, shoes and ties, and musically in a number of soul covers between Weller's own Who-echoing originals.

Familiar on the London live scene by mid-1976, the band toyed with, and then abandoned, the idea of finding a keyboards player to turn them into a four-piece. In a ploy to raise their profile, they did an impromptu alfresco gig at London's Soho market (plugging into power from the Rock On record stall), and duly got mentions in the music press and the notice of

The Clash, who happened to spot the performance. Rock On owner Ted Carroll's Chiswick label very nearly signed the trio, only to be beaten to the dotted line in February 1977 by Polydor's Chris Parry, who secured them with a reputed £6000 advance. Within three months, their debut 45 'In The City' (with the same title as an old Who B-side, but actually a Weller original) made the chart, peaking at No.40, and was followed immediately by the album of the same title, which made No.20 and took up a lengthy chart residency as the band launched into their first headline UK tour. Recorded in only 11 days, the album revealed Weller's polific writing ability – he penned every track apart from the jokey 'Batman' theme and the pounding Larry Williams oldie 'Slow Down'.

The rest of 1977 saw a flurry of almost hyper-activity. In August, 'All Around The World' gave the band their first Top 20 single, reaching No.13. Following tours in Europe and the US, they then had another (smaller) hit single, 'The Modern World' in November, with a second album, 'This Is The Modern World', hitting the Top 30 in its wake.

The Jam became the first act ever to chart three successive singles with 'world' in their titles when 'News Of The World' made the Top 30 in March 1978. It was followed by their only cover version A-side, in the shape of 'David Watts', originally a '60s album track by The Kinks,

penned by Ray Davies. This peaked at No.25, but was then eclipsed by Weller's own 'Down In The Tube Station At Midnight', a critically-rated song which brought the writer's social awareness to the fore as well as heralding a more tightly-produced – and now wholly original – Jam sound. This single made No.15, and also introduced an equally feted third album, 'All Mod Cons', which rapidly shot to a heady No.6 in the charts towards the end of 1978.

1979 saw two more Top 20 hits, 'Strange Town' and 'When You're Young', before 'The Eton Rifles' became their biggest single yet, hitting No.3 towards the end of the year. A barbed comment on institutionalised militarism, this also introduced 'Setting Sons', a near concept album which took equally sharp bites at assorted forms of established institution, and carried hints that Weller's 60s muse was now Ray Davies of The Kinks rather than The Who's Pete Townshend.

'Setting Sons' hit No.4, and was The Jam's biggest-selling album yet. In fact, after three years of constantly building popularity (a rarity in rock music in general, let alone among the ephemeral rush of the punk era), 1980 saw the band as one of the biggest in the UK – a notion supported by their hugely successful tours to packed audiences, and the fact that 'Going Underground' in March hit No.1 in its week of release, indicating a huge fanbase of committed buyers. Moreover, the band had not softened their musical approach by this time: there was more variety in arrangement and more complexity in the writing than at the beginning of their recording career, but most Jam tracks still flew on a burst of taut energy, with Weller's vocal bark undiminished. In a sense, the band who had never quite been punks at the beginning now shone the torch of the punk spirit more brightly than any other major act.

Still bigger commercial triumphs ensued, however. 'Start' (carried on an adaptation of The Beatles' 'Taxman' riff) was also a 1980 No.1 single, and the album 'Sound Affects' made No.2 at the end of the year. 1981 delivered two No.4 singles, 'Funeral Pyre' and 'Absolute Beginners', while even an import-only single, 'That's Entertainment' (extracted from 'Sound Affects') made No.21. In 1982, they finally scored a No.1 album with their sixth LP 'The Gift', following hot on the heels of another chart-topping single, the double A-side 'A Town Called Malice' and 'Precious'. This latter single also did well internationally, with 'Precious' denting the US dance market and 'Malice' charting in several countries. This did, however, point up the band's major career problem: little of their material had repeated anything like its UK success around the world, and certainly not in America, where The Jam enjoyed buoyant cult status, but only the minimal sales that this suggested. The notion that the band was in a kind of parochial tunnel on the same old track began to weigh upon Weller, always the driving force of The Jam as its main writer, singer and guitarist. He began to attribute the lack of widening international appeal to what he perceived as the musical straitjacket of The Jam's basic rock sound, and

started to look to his deeper soul and R&B influences for fresh inspiration, while also realising that the band could not make a wholesale, radical shift in musical style without losing the essence of what made them The Jam. The Top 10 hits continued to come during 1982 with 'Just Who Is The Five O'Clock Hero' and 'The Bitterest Pill (I Ever Had To Swallow)', and the band went all over the world on their Trans-Global Unity tour, but in October, Weller announced that The Jam had achieved everything it could, and would split at the end of the year after a final UK tour. Clearly, the motivation for the break-up was all his, but Foxton and Buckler recognised, pragmatically, that there was no way the band could survive without Weller anyway. In the event, they went out in style, and genuinely at their peak of popularity, as the last single 'Beat Surrender' was another instant No.1, the live compilation LP 'Dig The New Breed' (drawing from all stages of their career) hit No.2, and the farewell tour was a huge success, taking in six sold-out nights at Wembley Arena, and a triumphal final gig in the mod's symbolic centre of Brighton.

Within months, Weller had embarked upon the second successful stage of his career with The Style Council, a soul/funk-based outfit which satisfied his current vision of musical expansion for several more years. Both Foxton and Buckler also had initial solo success, though would find themselves unable to sustain the commercial momentum of their erstwhile partner: by the 1990s, the drummer would be concentrating on running his recording studio, and the bassist would have joined the re-formed Stiff Little Fingers. Meanwhile, in the years immediately following their dissolution, The Jam's recordings refused to lie down, Polydor's reissue of their singles en masse early in 1983 saw virtually the whole catalogue back in the chart, while later in the year, the double greatest hits compilation album 'Snap' reached No.2 and stayed charted for 30 weeks. Even 10 years after the split, 'Extras', a retrospective album of B-sides, rarities and unissued Jam material was able to whip up enough interest to chart at No.15.

Recommended CD listening: 'Snap' (Polydor 815 537-2) and 'In The City/This Is The Modern World' (Polydor 847 730-2)

JILTED JOHN

Graham Fellows, a Yorkshire-born, Manchester-based drama student, was the real person behind lovelorn loser Jilted John, whose eponymous single was punk's most successful excursion into parodic humour. The whining monologue over a breakneck instrumental track, with its gormless 'Gordon is a moron' chorus, was produced by 'Martin Zero' (actually Factory's Martin Hannett) for Manchester indie label Rabid in the spring of 1978, and sold in ever-increasing numbers, largely via word-of-mouth enthusiasm, until brought to the attention of EMI Records by the staff of *Record Business* magazine. EMI's reissue hit No.4, selling over a quarter of a million copies, and spawned 'True Love Stories', an album of similar novelties from the teenage wasteland, plus a couple of less successful answer- disc sequels from Gordon The Moron and Julie & Gordon.

Fellows himself, however, wisely stuck to acting after his taste of one-off hit making, and later had a role in *Coronation Street* and also featured in several idiosyncratic stage productions. A far more enduring character for him than Jilted John has been John Shuttleworth, another comedy/musical creation who has found success on stage and radio in the 1990s.

JUBILEE

Had punk come along in the mid-60s, when the British film industry was still prolific, it might easily have been the opportunistic focus of a whole bunch of bargain-basement movies cashing in on the music and the style, much as the British Beat Boom had been. Although there were a couple of later efforts (*Rude Boy* and *Breaking Glass*) set in the punk-orientated music business, it was Derek Jarman's 1978 film *Jubilee* which was to successfully freeze-frame all the trappings of punk circa 1977 in celebratory fashion for celluloid posterity.

Jarman used the fact that 1977, the year of The Sex Pistols' commercial breakthrough, was also the Jubilee year of Queen Elizabeth II (a point also not lost on The Pistols themselves, as evidenced by the controversial 'God Save The Queen' single, and the alternative Jubilee celebration of their River Thames boat stunt). Jarman's fantasy black comedy had Tudor monarch Elizabeth I zapping up the centuries to check out her successor's reign, and encountering a world taken over by punk, but much of this was a sideline to the film's musical content, which included contributions from Adam & The Ants, Siouxsie & The Banshees, Chelsea, and Wayne County's Electric Chairs, among others, all under the overall guidance of former Roxy Music avant-gardist Brian Eno. Such assorted luminaries as Jenny Runacre, Ian Charleson, Toyah Wilcox, Little Nell and Richard O'Brien figured among the cast.

KILLING JOKE

Killing Joke formed in mid-1979, and were never part of either the original UK punk explosion of its early-80s reprise, but the sonic assault approach of their style could probably only have developed and succeeded in the post-punk context, and they were certainly a vital part of the UK new wave. A quartet, they comprised Jaz Coleman (vocals and keyboards), K. 'Geordie' Walker (guitar), Martin 'Youth' Glover (bass) and Paul Ferguson (drums). Early appearances included support to The Ruts, while their vinyl debut, on Island, came in October 1979 with the three-track single 'Are You Receiving'/'Nervous System'/'Turn To Red'. In 1980, when they played with Joy Division, their own Malicious Damage label was launched (initially through Island, then via EG/Polydor), with the singles 'Wardance' and 'Requiem', and their eponymous debut album, which reached the Top 40 in November. Most of the band's material featured heavily aggressive instrumental work and hard-hitting lyrics, often anti-authoritarian or anti-military with a streak of wry, dark humour, and their style distanced them significantly from the yobbish anti-establishment ranks of the then-contemporary punk and Oi! waves.

From 1981's 'Follow The Leaders', they began to hit the national top 75, and a string of chart singles followed through to 1986, the biggest of which was 'Love Like Blood', a Top 20 success in February 1985. The albums 'Revelations' (1982) and 'Night Time' (1985) also made the Top 20. Even a peculiar hiatus early in 1992, when Jaz and Geordie suddenly upped and relocated in Iceland to play with a local band (supposedly because Coleman had become convinced that the Apocalypse was on its way) didn't stall the band's progress for too long, and they were together in one form or another through to the 1990 album 'Extremities, Dirt And Various Repressed Emotions', after which there was an ill-tempered split – though Coleman and Youth in particular would subsequently follow busy solo recording and production careers.

Recommended CD listening: 'Killing Joke' (Virgin EGCD 57)

KLEENEX

Among the more unlikely denizens of the late-70s punk world were this all-girl quartet from Zurich, Switzerland, formed in March 1978. Comprising Regula Sing (vocals), Marlene Marder (guitar), Klaudia Schiff (bass) and Lisolt Ha (drums), they debuted on record in the Autumn of that year with the 500-copy limited-edition EP 'Beri-Beri', on the Sunrise label. In 1979, after drawing comparisons sound-wise with Siouxsie & The Banshees, they signed to Rough Trade in the UK and Sing departed, to be replaced by Chrigel Freund, former lead vocalist with another Euro-punk band, Chaos. Moderately successful Rough Trade releases, helped by regular gigs in the UK (they found it difficult to get any exposure in Switzerland), included the singles 'Ain't You' and 'You' in 1979, and 'Split' in 1980, and a cassette-only live album titled 'Die Kleenex Spielen', also during early 1980.

Midway through this year, the band suddenly changed their name to Liliput, presumably under pressure from the Kleenex paper tissue company, but the line-up and recording deal were unaltered. Liliput's handful of releases in 1981 and '82, however, meant comparatively little, and the quartet faded from view, at least in the UK, under the domestic onslaught of the new punk wave.

Killing Joke

Some of the Jubilee contingent

Greetings *from London*

LEYTON BUZZARDS

This quartet, formed in 1976 in Leyton, East London, by vocalist Geoff Deane and bassist David Jaymes, and augmented by Dave Monk on guitar And Kevin Steptoe on drums, began as a pub R&B band, but adapted their style to get gigs at London's new punk clubs. In 1978, after appearing on EMI's 'Live At The Roxy' compilation, they signed the customary one-single deal with Small Wonder Records, and in July released the three-track effort '19 And Mad'/ 'Villain'/ 'Euthanasia' - songs which demonstrated their full adoption of the punk idiom (as did the pseudonyms they assumed for this single – Deane became Nick Nayme, James was Dave DePrave, Monk amended himself to Chip Monk, and Steptoe became Gray Mare).

With new guitarist Vernon Austin in place of Monk, the band won a Radio 1-sponsored competition for unsigned bands, and got a deal with Chrysalis as their prize, resulting in the single 'Saturday Night (Beneath The Plastic Palm Trees)', a celebration of riotous living which charted nationally at No.53 early in 1979. Two more Chrysalis singles failed to make the grade, however, even though on the second, 'We Make A Noise', the band shortened their name to The Buzzards in order to signify a new direction. They split at the end of 1979, though by little more than a year later, Deane and Jaymes had re-invented themselves, with new accompanying musicians, as the Latin-dance-orientated (and soon to be very successful) Modern Romance.

Leyton Buzzards

LONDON S.S.

The London S.S. were the seminal UK punk outfit that never really was – in the sense that the band never settled upon a complete line-up, played any gigs or released any records. Nevertheless, they can be fairly considered as the main wellspring of much of London's punk talent in the mid-1970s, since so many of the key players were first made aware of each other through the attempts of the S.S. to get it together as a group.

From March 1975, the principal movers were guitarist Mick Jones and bassist Tony James, who spent until the end of the year trying out other musicians who shared their vision of a fired-up young band with the best elements of The MC5, The New York Dolls and Iggy & The Stooges. The

first successful recruit was another guitarist, Bryan James, but a round of endless basement rehearsals and auditions followed, while a mere couple of miles away The Sex Pistols were pulling themselves together from much less promising material, and graduating in November to actual gigs.

The trio almost got it together (and made a demo tape with) drummer Roland Hot, but Bryan James eventually tired of all the hanging around, and split in January 1976 to form The Damned with Rat Scabies (whom the S.S. had not wanted). This prompted Mick Jones to cut his own losses and link with Joe Strummer of The 101-ers to start The Clash, along with Terry Chimes and Paul Simenon – who had also both auditioned for (and been rejected by) London S.S. Tony James held down a day job for a few months, then formed Chelsea with Billy Idol and Gene October – which would in turn metamorphose into Generation X. Other London S.S. tryouts Casino Steel and Matt Dangerfield would form The Boys, while Nicky Headon – who, just to be different had turned down the drummer's job with the S.S. although they had wanted him – would settle into The Clash as Terry Chimes' replacement early in 1977.

LENE LOVICH

A key member of the late-1970s Stiff Records roster, Lene Lovich, like her sometime label-mate Elvis Costello, was an artist whose work did not strictly fall under a punk heading, but relied on the new open attitude of the punk audience to get a hearing and find commercial success.

Lovich's exotic, gypsy-like visual image deliberately obscured her origins, which were suggested as central European (the title of her first album, 'Stateless', further compounded the wilful vagueness), but she was in fact born in Detroit, USA, to a Yugoslav father and an English mother, and lived in London from her early teens. She studied at art school, became involved in musical theatre, and finally found her way to rock music after co-fronting a soul band named The Diversions with fellow ex-art student Les Chappell, who was to be her main collaborator and eventual husband. A flirtation with disco in Paris saw the duo pen a couple of hits for French disco artist Cerrone, after which they returned to the UK in the thick of the first punk eruption, and Lovich was signed by Stiff during 1978, joining the other mainstays of the roster on the high-profile Be Stiff tour of the UK and (briefly) the US. This helped the 'Stateless' album along (it eventually made No.35), but she was not to taste major chart success until the beginning of 1979, when she scooped massive radio play and hit UK No.3 with the catchy post-punk rocker 'Lucky Number', selling over a quarter million copies. 'Say When' and 'Bird Song' followed it into the Top 40, while her second album 'Flex' reached No.19 in February 1980.

Further minor hits followed through 1982, but she was suffering strained relations with Stiff, and her third album 'No Man's Land' lived up to the label's name. While continuing to occasionally perform in concert, she concentrated her activities on songwriting, films (she appeared in the continental films *Cha Cha* and *Rock*) and a return to musical theatre (she scored and appeared in *Mata Hari* in London's West End).

Recommended CD listening: 'Stiff Years, Vol.1' (Great Expectations PIPCD

PUNK!

LIVE STIFFS GREATEST STIFFS

WRECKLESS ERIC NICK LOWE ELVIS COSTELLO LARRY WALLIS IAN DURY

WHERE THE FUN NEVER SETS

STIFF RECORDS

DUMPING MUSIC ON THE PEOPLE AT

October

6 Bristol Exhibition Centre

7 Bath University

8 Loughborough University

9 Middlesborough Town Hall

11 Liverpool Empire

13 Glasgow Apollo

14 Sheffield Polytechnic

15 Leeds University

16 Fairfield Halls Croydon

18 University of East Anglia, Norwich

19 Brighton Top Rank

21 Salford University

22 Leicester University

24 Champness Hall Rochdale

25 Birmingham Town Hall

26 Cardiff Top Rank

27 Wolverhampton Civil Hall

28 Lyceum London

31 Guildford Civic

November

2 Friars Aylesbury

3 Essex University

4 Newcastle Polytechnic

5 Lancaster University

PUNK!

A Lurking Howard Wall

THE LURKERS

Fulham, West London's Lurkers, a foursome comprising Howard Wall (vocals), Pete Stride (guitar), Arturo Bassick (bass – replaced after 10 months briefly by Kym Bradshaw, and then by Tony Moore) and Esso (Pete Haynes) (drums) were cheerful punk minimalists who mastered the art of the sharp, spiky, commercial single very quickly. Aided by the astute marketing of small label Beggars Banquet (to which they were the first signings, in August 1977), they managed, after an initial couple of misses, to chart a whole string of singles – five, including 'I Don't Need To Tell Her'/'Pills' and 'Just Thirteen' – across an 18-month period during 1978/79, which was a better score than all but an elite few 70s punk bands. What did elude, them, however, was a really big hit: their top seller 'Ain't Got A Clue' only managed to reach No.45, while their one chart album 'Fulham Fallout', released at the same time in the summer of 1978, peaked at 57. It featured additional member Pete Edwards (harmonica and backing vocals), and was highlighted by the band's humorous take on a classic Phil Spector number as 'Then I Kicked Her'.

The band's 1979 and 1980 albums 'God's Lonely Men' and 'King Of The Mountain' fared less well, as the Ramones-like simplicity of their style seemed to have run its commercial course by then. When 'Honest' John Plain (previously with The Boys) joined them in October 1979, in time for the appropriately-titled single 'New Guitar In Town', the good times were all but gone: this was their last chart entry, at a modest No.72. The Lurkers disbanded during the early 1980s, but they would eventually reform for punk nostalgia shows a decade later.

Recommended CD listening: 'Totally Lurkered' (Dojo CD 74)

ANARCHY IN THE U.K. TOUR

SEX PISTOLS

FIRST MAJOR U.K. TOUR WITH SPECIAL GUESTS

THE DAMNED

JOHNNY THUNDER'S HEART BREAKERS
(Ex New York Dolls from USA)

THE CLASH

TOUR DATES

		Tickets From
FRI 3 DEC	NORWICH University	Students Union, U.E.A.
SAT 4 DEC	DERBY Kings Hall	Kings Hall, Derby
		R.E. Cords, Derby, Burton Slect a Disc
SUN 5 DEC	NEWCASTLE City Hall	Nottingham Record Centre, Long Eaton
MON 6 DEC	LEEDS Polytechnic	City Hall
TUE 7 DEC	BOURNEMOUTH	Village Bowl
	Village Bowl	Students Union, Leeds Poly
THU 9 DEC	MANCHESTER	Hime & Adamson, Manchester
	Electric Circus	Virgin Records, Manchester
FRI 10 DEC	LANCASTER University	
SAT 11 DEC	LIVERPOOL Stadium	Students Union, Lancaster University
MON 13 DEC	BRISTOL Colston Hall	Virgin Records
TUE 14 DEC	CARDIFF Top Rank	Top Rank, Cardiff
		Buffalo Records
WED 15 DEC	GLASGOW Apollo	Colston Hall
THU 16 DEC	DUNDEE Caird Hall	Apollo, Glasgow
		Caird Hall
FRI 17 DEC	SHEFFIELD City Hall	Students Union, Technical College
SAT 18 DEC	SOUTHEND Kursaal	City Hall – Wilson Peck Records
SUN 19 DEC	GUILDFORD Civic Hall	Usual Agents
MON 20 DEC	BIRMINGHAM Town Hall	Usual Agents
TUE 21 DEC	PLYMOUTH Woods Centre	Town Hall
		Virgin Records
WED 22 DEC	TORQUAY 400 Ballroom	Woods Centre
SUN 26 DEC	LONDON Roxy Theatre Harlesden	400 Club
		Roxy Theatre

SINGLES AVAILABLE

THE DAMNED. NEW ROSE   HELP (BUY 6)
Available from even your dumbest dealer
SEX PISTOLS. ANARCHY IN THE U.K. (EMI 2566)
Available from your cleverest

TOUR PRESENTED BY ENDALE ASSOCIATES
IN ARRANGEMENT WITH MALCOLM MACLAREN

MALCOLM McLAREN

Malcolm McLaren may be regarded as the single most important figure in the birth of the original punk movement in Britain, on the basis that The Sex Pistols came into being directly as a result of a McLaren concept, and were it not for the presence and influence of The Pistols, it is unlikely that the genre would have mushroomed into being at all, or whether some of its key bands would ever have been inspired to get together.

McLaren's involvement with the Pistols is chronicled in detail in the band's own entry later in this book, but his story, and the relevant background to his role as punk's major svengali, goes much further back. Hailing from a middle-class but somewhat dysfunctional family background, which probably accounted for his obsessive and sometimes contradictory personality, he was an art student through most of the latter half of the

1960s, studying at Harrow Art School, Croydon Art College (where he met designer Jamie Reid) and Goldsmith's College (where he studied film and photography). In 1867, he also began a long-running relationship with fellow art student and designer Vivienne Westwood, who was to become his professional as well as personal partner during the early '70s. It was while he was a student that McLaren also became interested in fringe aspects of radical politics — not in any political ends as such, but in their use of conceptualised situations, sloganeering, and pop-culture crossover. Such notions would inform his thinking during later entrepreneural days.

Late in 1971, McLaren and Westwood took over the use of a former boutique at 430, Kings Road, and turned it into Let It Rock, a shop catering for the 50s revival fad. They sold rare records and memorabilia from the

era, plus customised T-shirts and leather jackets, and 'genuine' teddy boy shoes and clothing, much of the latter made by Westwood. For a while, this found a profitable niche in a large but previously untapped market, and a huge clientele of both original and nouveau-teds were regular patrons. The shop was also commissioned to provide the costumes for the film *That'll Be The Day*, set in the teenage 1950s and starring David Essex and Ringo Starr.

Eventually, McLaren tired of the one-dimensionality of his customers, and in order to attract a wider spread, he and Westwood changed the shop in the Spring of 1973 to Too Fast To Live, Too Young To Die, and as well as the rocker gear, moved into Zoot suits and other retro-hip creations. In the same year, the pair were offered the chance to display their idiosyncratic range at the National Boutique Show in New York, and it was there, while mystifying American fashion journalists at the McAlpin hotel, that McLaren encountered The New York Dolls, then a major Manhattan club rage who had just finally got their dreamed-of recording contract with Mercury. The Dolls were interested in McLaren's way-out garb, but he was even more mesmerised by the band's energy, hedonism, ability to project a don't-care attitude as pure stylishness, and the exciting sense of imminent possibility that they carried around with them. On his return to London, he kept in touch with The Dolls, and linked up with them again when they did a UK and European tour at the end of 1973. He became interested in the background machinations of the rock industry, regularly pumping *NME* writer Nick Kent for information, and developed an obsession with the early example of Britain's original rock'n'roll svengali, Larry Parnes.

By early 1974, McLaren and Westwood decided the shop needed to move on again. They closed Too Fast To Live in April, and began to convert it into what would become Sex, focusing on rubber and other fetish wear, though inevitably with the sort of modifications – slogans, studs and so on – which already characterised their style, and which would hopefully turn what was normally thought of as sexual clothing into adventurous young street wear, available to all.

During 1974, McLaren was also approached by one of his customers, a teenage would-be guitarist named Steve Jones, who was trying to get a band working with his mates Paul Cook and Warwick Nightingale. He found some rehearsal space for them, and generally left them to his mate

Bernie Rhodes to oversee, and this motley crew would eventually become the embryonic roots of The Sex Pistols.

When McLaren returned to New York at the end of the year, he found The New York Dolls in post-second-album disarray and fragmented by drugs and alcohol. For a while, he became their ad hoc manager, his main accomplishment being to reinvent them in a new visual image of startling red leather. This backfired badly on tour when the hammer & sickle introduced as a logo drew inevitable US anti-communist wrath down upon the band. In the Spring of 1975 they broke up, and after he and The Dolls' Sylvain Sylvain had failed to reconstruct the band with new musicians, McLaren came back to London to check out Jones' band instead.

The creation of The Sex Pistols out of initially unpromising material is told in The Pistols' story in this book, and of course, it made McLaren a public *enfant terrible* in his own right. Sex, the shop, also prospered during the anarchic early punk boom, though not always without its hassles, such as a highly subsidised bust over allegedly obscene T-shirts.

After the *Great Rock'n'Roll Swindle* movie closed the Sex Pistols period in appropriate (and literal) wide-screen tawdriness, McLaren tried again from the beginning, as it were, by manufacturing a new band out of enforced fragmentation of Adam & The Ants (ie, he fired Adam). Bow Wow Wow, the band made up from the remnants and fronted by exotic schoolgirl Annabella L'win, were ripe for his by now typically mercurial style of manipulation, and initially very successful, but in the long run he probably backed the wrong horse, since Adam plus his replacement group of Ants became one of the biggest pop sensations of the early 80s. It marked the close of McLaren's involvement with punk – which in any case was melting rapidly into the mainstream (or resurfacing in forms, like Oi!, that he failed to relate to) by the time of Bow Wow Wow. From 1983 (also the year in which he and Westwood finally split, somewhat acrimoniously), he was to to make his least expected move yet, and re-invent himself as a hitmaking act in his own right – not as a singer or musician as such (he could not sing or play anything), but as an organiser, arranger, marketer and front man of, in turn, African tribal music, New York-style street dance, and cod-opera. No stone, as ever, was to remain unturned for the man whose enthusiasm for slogans, concepts and 'situations' had given the world the snotty, angry, spiteful one called punk .

PUNK!

Howard Devoto of Magazine

MAGAZINE

When Howard Devoto left The Buzzcocks in February 1977, he considered resuming his college studies and perhaps pursuing musical projects on the side. In fact, he began working quietly with guitarist John McGeoch on new songs within a matter of weeks, and they started to formulate a band in contrast to The Buzzcocks' high-energy approach of which Devoto had so tired. By August 1977, Magazine was assembled, comprising Devoto and McGeoch plus Bob Dickinson (keyboards, for the first four months only, then replaced by Dave Formula), Barry Adamson (bass) and Martin Jackson (drums), and they played their first gig at the final night of Manchester's Electric Circus club (alongside The Buzzcocks) in October.

Signing with Virgin in January 1978, the band immediately charted with the critically-acclaimed single 'Shot By Both Sides', although it could only peak at No.41 – possibly because they refused to mime it on *Top Of The Pops*, and so didn't make the programme. The debut album 'Real Life', also the subject of rave reviews, reached the top 30 in July, and would be emulated over the next two years by 'Secondhand Daylight' (which received their first negative coverage) and 'The Correct Use Of Soap', but the band found less luck with follow-up singles, and had just one more minor chartmaker with 'Sweet Heart Contract' in mid-1980. As a live act, they proved in constant demand, touring North America in 1979 and again (plus Australasia) in 1980, as well as several UK treks. In mid-1980, they lost McGeoch, who began to play with the seriously guitarist-less Siouxsie & The Banshees between Magazine tours, and never came back. Former Ultravox guitarist Robin Simon replaced him for the 1980 overseas sojurns (on which were recorded the Christmas-released live album 'Play'), while by now John Doyle had also taken over on drums from Jackson. At the beginning of 1981, a new guitarist, Devoto's long-time friend Ben

Mandelson, was hired to play on sessions for the next album, 'Magic, Murder And The Weather', and stayed on as a full-time member. By now, however, Devoto was feeling the on-the-road pressure all over again: in May, just three weeks before the album's release, he announced that he was unwilling to tour to promote it, and had decided to leave the band. Although it was not his intention to disband Magazine as well, the other members, recognising Devoto's pivotal role, decided that there was no future for the band without him. The final album charted two weeks after Magazine ceased to exist.

Recommended CD listening: 'Rays And Hail 1978-81 (The Best Of Magazine)' (Virgin COMCD 5)

MAX'S KANSAS CITY

Along with CBGB's and the Mercer Arts Centre, Max's Kansas City, on Park Avenue South at 17th Street, was one of the key clubs in Manhattan in the early 1970s where the acts who either strongly influenced, or became an integral part of, the American new wave of punk, first unleashed themselves on the New York audience. Max's had rock connections back to The Velvet Underground in the mid-late 1960s, and several of The Velvets' alternative culture inheritors also inevitably graced its stage, including The New York Dolls, Television, Wayne County, Patti Smith, Pere Ubu and Sylvain Sylvain's post-Dolls band The Criminals. Unlike CBGB's, however, (though like the Mercer, which physically collapsed along with the old building containing it) Max's failed to survive the changing fashions of the late 1970s, and was defunct by the time the new music explosion became a commercial reality in America at the end of the decade.

PUNK!

Above: Wayne County & The Electric Chairs playing at Max's Kansas City
Right: Blondie's Chris Stein and Debbie Harry on stage at Max's

THE MEKONS

Arguably Leeds' most significant contribution to the punk scene was this larger-than-usual aggregation, drawing on two vocalists (Andy Carrigan and Mark White), two guitarists (Kevin Lycett and Tom Greenhalgh), Ross Allen on bass and Jon Langford on drums. They debuted their enthusiastic DIY style for Bob Last's Edinburgh-based indie label Fast Product in February 1978, producing the single 'Never Been In A Riot', followed at the end of the year by 'Where Were You?'. These releases led to a deal with Virgin, which saw two more singles over the next 18 months, plus the album 'The Quality Of Mercy Is Not Strnen', which received good critical comment but not a lot in the way of sales – probably the reason why the band found themselves back in the indie sector, with the Red Rhino single 'Snow', before the end of 1980. Their profile reduced considerably at this time, and line-up changes began to set in, largely out of the general public eye, but the band itself did not split once the rock press coverage ceased: there was, on average, a Mekons album a year through until the early 90s, embracing a wider musical canvas, but always fuelled by the forthright by-our-own-bootstraps ethic which had driven the band from the beginning.
Recommended CD listening: 'The Quality Of Mercy Is Not Strnen' (Virgin CDV 2143)

PUNK!

THE MEMBERS

Somewhat unfashionably when they formed in 1977, The Members did not originate from a harsh inner city, but from the prosperous commuter belt surroundings of Camberley, Surrey – lead vocalist Nicky Tesco even had a daytime job when he put the band together – he was a university-educated insurance salesman! With a line-up that also included Jean-Marie Carroll (guitar and chief songwriter), Gary Baker (guitar), Chris Payne (bass) and Adrian Lillywhite (drums), The Members played their first live gig at London's Roxy club in July 1977, recorded 'Fear On The Streets' for Beggars Banquet's punk compilation LP 'Streets'), and then got a one-record deal with Stiff, which produced their first single, 'Solitary Confinement' (released, appropriately, on the 1-Off subsidiary label). At this point, in Spring 1978, Baker left, and Nigel Bennett came in on guitar.

In November 1978, the band signed to Virgin and hit their commercial streak, all the while refining what had originally been a very basic punk sound into a spiky synthesis of rock and reggae destined to characterise much of their work. A national tour supporting Devo provided excellent promotion for the debut Virgin single 'The Sound Of The Suburbs', and aided by a transparent vinyl pressing and special packaging, it climbed to an impressive No.12 in February 1979, to be followed two months later by 'Offshore Banking Business', which peaked at 31, and the band's first album, 'At The Chelsea Nightclub', which charted at No.45.

By the second half of 1979, the band's chart career was, surprisingly, over, with three further Virgin singles and a second album, '1980 – The Choice Is Yours', failing to make the grade. Band and label consequently parted, and during 1981/2, The Members turned up on independents Albion and Genetic, the former label releasing their final album 'Going West', and the latter the single 'Radio', which gave them a surprise hit in Australasia. Beyond this, however, lay obscurity, and the band split before the end of 1963.

Recommended CD listening: 'Sounds Of The Suburbs - A Collection Of The Members' Finest Moments' (Virgin CDOVD 455)

THE MO-DETTES

One of the few all-girl punk bands to make much of a commercial showing, the Mo-Dettes, formed early in 1979, were a quartet with varied roots. Guitarist Kate Corris was from the US, though had lived in London since 1974, and played in the earliest incarnation of The Slits in 1977. Bassist Jane Crockford, a former teenage runaway, had shared a squat with Sid Vicious and Johnny Rotten, and first played her instrument briefly in Bank Of Dresden, before becoming a Mo-Dette. Vocalist Ramona Carlier was a former ballet student from Geneva, in the French-speaking part of Switzerland (her French language influences were used on some of the band's material, like a cover of 'Milord'), and had moved to London

because of Switzerland's total lack of punk culture. Drummer June Miles-Kingston first met Corris on the set of The Sex Pistols' film *The Great Rock'n'Roll Swindle*, where both were employed as background musicians.

The group's first and most highly-regarded release was the self-penned 'White Mice', released in mid-1979 on their own Rough Trade-distributed Mode label. A steady seller on the back of a busy round of club gigs, it was still a top five indie single when the official independent chart was launched in February 1980, and was instrumental in gaining the quartet signed to Decca's Deram label. A cover of The Rolling Stones' 'Paint It Black', a long-time stage favourite, launched this deal and made No.42 in the national chart, but the album 'The Story So Far' which followed it got poor reviews (mostly lambasting weak, unsympathetic production), and with this the girls seemingly began to run out of steam, scoring just one more minor hit with 'Tonight' in mid-1981 before Carlier left, disillusioned, six months later. New singer Sue Slack came in, and they experimented with a more commercial approach with producer Chris Neil, but then Corris left too, and the heart effectively went out of the group: it disbanded within months. Jane Crockford married Dan Woodgate of Madness, while June Miles-Kingston would eventually re-emerge in the late 80s as the girl drummer with The Communards.

MONT DE MARSAN PUNK FESTIVAL

The close quarters, the in-your-face nature of punk rock and the celebratory tribal atmosphere of the traditional big-scale outdoor rock festival seem a rather unlikely mixture. The connection was made, however – sort of – on one occasion, when on August 28th 1976, the Mont De Marsan bullring, in the South of France between Bordeaux and the Pyrenees, hosted The First European Punk Rock Festival. It was an event promoted by Marc Zermati, whose label Skydog Records had made an early commitment to punk (and pub-rock, with a Gallic inability to apparently distinguish the two!) on the Continent. Zermati's original bill for the festival had it head-lined by The Sex Pistols, The Clash, Richard Hell & The Voidoids and Graham Parker & The Rumour, but all of these, for a variety of reasons, eventually pulled out. The roster which actually played was a curious mixture of punk and R&B/pub-rock bands: Eddie & The Hot Rods, Nick Lowe, The Pink Fairies, Sean Tyler & The Tyler Gang, The Hammersmith Gorillas, The Count Bishops and The Damned (playing only their fifth gig), plus a number of French outfits that included Little Bob Story, Bijoux, Shakin' Street and Il Baritz. The Hot Rods topped the bill triumphantly (typically, for an outdoor festival, at about two in the morning), while The Damned were acknowledged as making the biggest audience impression of any of the new, untried acts. Unfortunately, nothing of the now-legendary event was ever recorded for posterity.

Modettes

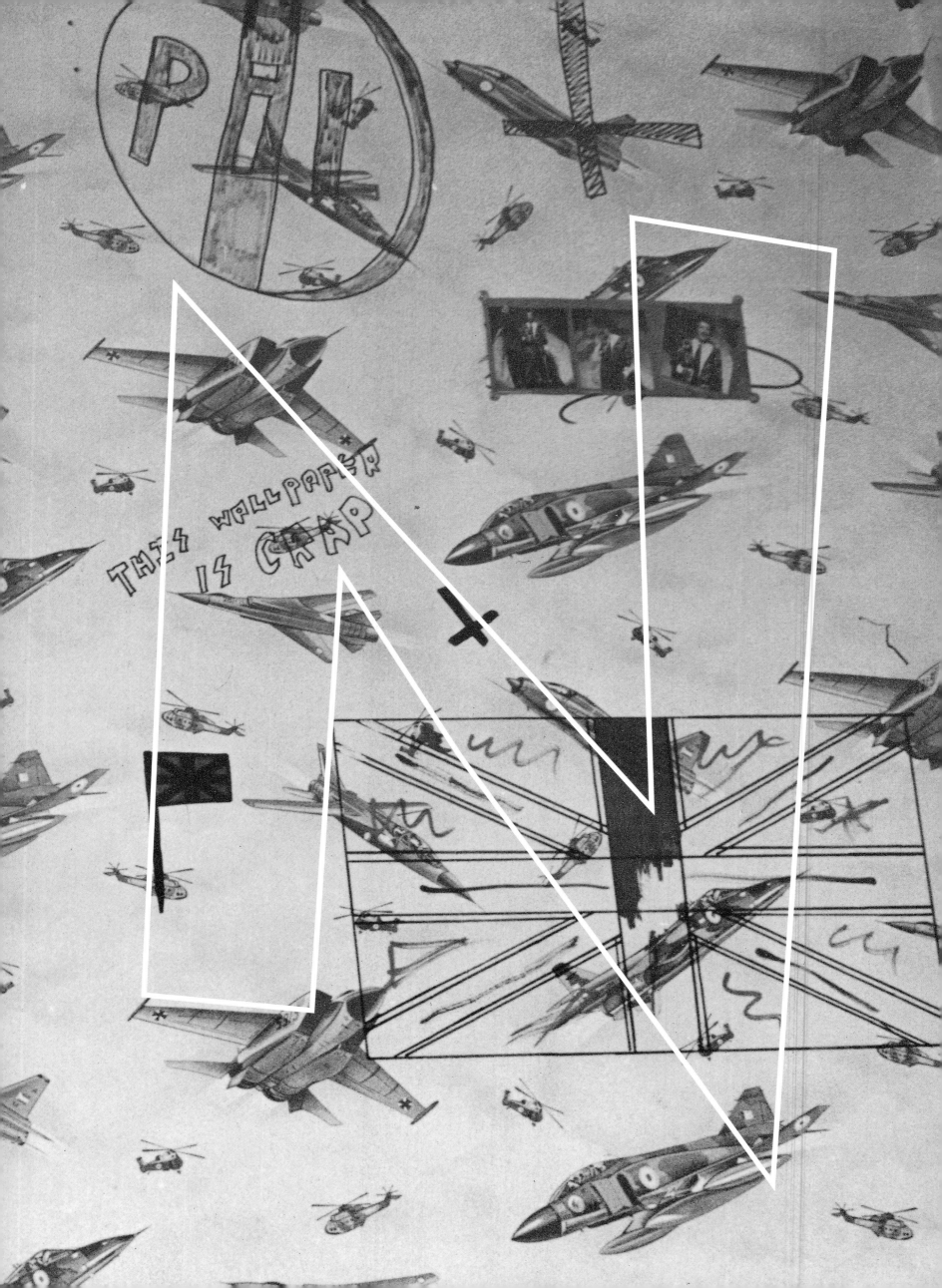

THE NEW YORK DOLLS

On the face of it an unsuccessful and not particularly long-lived rock band of the early 1970s, The New York Dolls were – after they had broken up – to prove highly influential on the emerging punk scenes of both the US and UK a handful of years later, more due to their high energy level and rebellious, nonconformist demeanour than a specific carry-over of musical style. Also significant is the fact that, following their first visit to London, Malcolm McLaren became enamoured of their image and for a while in 1975 took over as their manager, absorbing much which he sought to recreate with The Sex Pistols a couple of years later.

The Dolls formed in New York City in January 1972, the early line-up comprising David Johansen (vocals), Johnny Thunders (vocals and guitar), Sylvain Sylvain (guitar – replaced Rick Rivets, who was only in for two months), Arthur Kane (bass) and Billy Murcia (drums). Early gigs at clubs like the Mercer Arts Center in Manhattan got them wide media coverage and enthusiasm, and they travelled to London to support The Faces – a visit tragically truncated when Murcia overdosed and died. Jerry Nolan stepped in on drums, and the new line-up was signed to Mercury, releasing two Albums: 'New York Dolls' in the Summer of 1973, and 'Too Much Too Soon' twelve months later. Both had 'name' producers (Todd Rundgren and Shadow Morton, respectively), and the first in particular was well reviewed, but neither sold particularly well, and partly because of their lack of record success the band failed to push their unique mixture of Rolling Stones/garage band music and over-the-top tacky image (including heavy makeup, and later all-red fetishistic stage outfits, courtesy of McLaren) to audiences outside their New York club heartland. Thunders and Nolan left, disillusioned, in May 1975, to then re-emerge with Richard Hell in The Heartbreakers. Johansen kept a version of The Dolls on the road gigging for another 18 months, with Peter Jordan taking over from Kane, who was

attempting to crack a drink problem. They played a highly lucrative tour of Japan in the latter half of 1975, but otherwise the band continued on a clear hiding to nowhere, and eventually disbanded in January 1977. Most of the key members started solo careers and/or new bands as the punk era proper kicked in, but (with the partial exception of Johnny Thunders' Heartbreakers) it curiously bypassed them all, at least commercially. Johansen would have the highest-profile career in the 80s and beyond, recording and performing both under his own name and as a semi-spoof alter-ego: the drink-fuelled R&B lounge performer Buster Poindexter.
Recommended CD listening: 'Live In NYC 1975 – Red Patent Leather' (Receiver RRCD 173)

999

999 came into being in May 1977, when the Northampton-originated, London-based band comprising Nick Cash (guitar and vocals – formerly with Ian Dury in Kilburn & The High Roads), Guy Days (guitar), Jon Watson (bass) and Pablo LaBritian (drums) changed their name from 48 Hours in hope of better things. Four months later, they released their debut single 'I'm Alive' on their own LaBritian label, positive reaction to which prompted United Artists to both pick up the disc and sign the band. Further urgent, snappy singles like 'Nasty Nasty', 'Emergency' and 'Me And My Desire' got good press without charting, and the band's first hit record was their debut LP '999' in March 1978. Curiously, subsequent albums would fail to chart, while their singles would start to register – beginning with 'Homicide' in December 1978, which, pressed on gimmicky green vinyl, was the band's only Top 40 entry, from the second (Martin Rushent-produced) album 'Separates'. They toured extensively overseas, and made a live

Left: Vocalist Nick Cash fronts 999

name for themselves in Europe and the US, as well as in Britain.

A car accident injury in the spring of 1979 put LaBritian out of action for a while, and Ed Case took over on drums. This also coincided with a parting of the ways from UA, and the band moved briefly to Radar Records in time for the minor hit single 'Found Out Too Late', before signing a deal with Polydor in January 1980. This produced the album 'The Biggest Prize In Sport', generally regarded as their best, but nonetheless not a big seller. Two more small single hits, though, came in 1981 when the band transferred to yet another label, Albion. Both 'Li'l Red Riding Hood' and 'Indian Reservation' were covers of pop oldies, suggesting that their punk roots (and once-abundant original material) had been left behind. However, the band did not split (though Watson was replaced by Danny Palmer a couple of years later), and with overseas popularity still intact, they continued to perform and record (without further commercial success) through the 1980s.

Recommended CD listening: 'Lust, Power And Money' (ABC ABCD 11)

THE NIPS

Initially comprising London-born but Irish-raised Shane MacGowan (vocals, as Shane O'Holligan), Roger Towndrow (guitar), Shanne Bradley (bass) and Jerry Arcane (drums), this quartet formed in London in the latter half of 1977. They were initially The Nipple Erectors, a name calculated to get them some press coverage (which it did), but also a likely barrier to live work among the easily-offended (as it also proved to be). Faced with the choice of keeping the name or working, the band took the pragmatic route and simply truncated themselves to The Nips.

The first act on indie label Soho Records, their initial release (as The Nipple Erectors) was the rockabilly-punk hybrid of 'King Of The Bop'/'Nervous Wreck' in June 1978. Three months later, the re-christened Nips returned with 'All The Time In The World', after which it was the best part of a year before they returned, in a new line-up (Towndrow and Arcane had departed, to be replaced by Stan Brennan and Gavin Douglas), with their biggest-selling single, the rousingly commercial 'Gabrielle'. This was still registering on the new indie charts at the start of 1980, but although it prompted the release of the Nips' only (and now hard-to-find) album, 'Only At The End Of The Beginning', it didn't herald long-term success for the band, because, splitting from Soho, they were not to resurface again until late in 1981, when Burning Rome's Test Pressing subsidiary released the obscure single 'Happy Song' – by the time of which, The Nips clearly realised that their punk moment had passed. McGowan moved on to join a short-lived outfit named The Chainsaws, but within two years would have re-invented himself as the carousing lead singer of Irish folk-punk minstrels The Pogues.

THE NORMIL HAWAIIANS

Why they were the 'Normil' and not 'Normal' Hawaiians was never made very clear (they claimed they simply couldn't spell), but this 1979-formed quintet comprising Guy Smith (vocals & guitar), Janet Armstrong (vocals), Jim Lusted (guitar), Nick (bass) and Brian Keelie (drums) weren't Hawaiians either, but came from Kent. Their first single was 'The Beat Goes On' for Dining Out Records in 1980, after which they label-hopped like nobody's business, releasing the 5-track EP 'Gala Failed' on Red Rhino a year later, and 'Still Obedient' on Illuminated at the end of 1981. None of these were big sellers, and the original line-up splintered early in 1982 (Janet Armstrong went off as a soloist and sessioneer, and was the female vocalist on David Bowie's 1986 'Absolute Beginners' single). Smith was left with the band name, and assembled a new Normil Hawaiians which comprised himself, Simon Marchant (guitar), Wilf Williams (bass) and Noel Blanden (drums). The band hardly ever played live, but recorded two albums for Illuminated – 'More Wealth Than Money' in 1983, and 'What's Going On?' in 1984 – before they retired to a part-time existence which played second fiddle to the members' other projects: Guy Smith actually become a circus performer!

NOTSENSIBLES

Notsensibles (they preferred it without a 'the') were from Burnley, Lancashire – close enough to Manchester to be affected by that city's 1977 explosion of punk bands, labels and lifestyle, the most prolific in the land outside London. Duly influenced, this teenage youth club quintet, with Haggis (vocals), Sage (guitar), Roger (keyboards), Gary (bass) and Kevin (drums) started on the Northern club circuit in 1979, initially performing covers, but quickly evolving a repertoire of their own which fitted their shambolic, good-time, always-see-the-funny-side nature. Notsensibles, as their name attested, were one of the new wave's comparative minority of compulsive piss-takers, zeroing in on absurdity where other bands shouted anger or balefully stared down their audience. Their second single and biggest success 'I'm In Love With Margaret Thatcher' (Top 10 in the indie chart early in 1980) exemplified the approach – a ludicrous concept allied to an eager, singalong, rock-pop sensibility. Given major distribution and wider promotion than the mere word-of-mouth of the indie-label circuit, it could easily have been a major national hit. As it happened, Notsensibles stuck to small labels (of the more offbeat kind, like Bent and Snotty Snail) and the solid support of their core fanbase, but several more singles and the album 'Instant Classic' kept their popularity rolling on for a couple of years, all featuring the band's highly original wry humour disguised as musical ineptitude, on titles like 'Death To Disco' and 'I Make A Balls Of Everything I Do'.

Recommended CD listening: 'Instant Punk Classics' (Anagram CD PUNK 38)

THE ONLY ONES

The Only Ones were formed in South London in 1976 by vocalist/guitar
Peter Perrett, who, via auditions, recruited three experienced musicians:
John Perry (guitar, ex-Ratbites From Hell), Alan Mair (bass, a veteran from
Scots favourites the Beatstalkers), and Mike Kellie (drums, formerly with the
V.I.P.'s, Peter Frampton and Spooky Tooth). Perrett himself had led the
Velvet Underground-styled England's Glory between 1972-74, and his Lou
Reed-like vocal persona was to carry over into the new band. Their record
debut was the single 'Lovers Of Today', released in July 1977 on their own
Vengeance label, reaction to which was sufficiently strong to see them
signed to CBS in the following January, by which time they had developed
a strong gigging presence on the punk circuit. In April 1978, while they
were touring as support to Television, the single 'Another Girl, Another
Planet' appeared, followed in May by the band's eponymous debut album.
Despite ecstatic reviews and wide airplay, the single failed to chart, though
the album made a brief appearance at No.56. This set a pattern whereby
their records were highly rated by the press, and they toured successfully
(including two US sojourns in 1978 and '79), but could not gain any large
scale hits or the wider mainstream success that would accompany them.

The second album 'Even Serpents Shine' reached No.42 in 1979, and
the third, 'Baby's Got A Gun', was The Only Ones' most successful record,
climbing to No.37 in the Spring of 1980. Still the singles failed, however,
as internal dissents, as well as friction with CBS, began to rock the band.
After being dropped by the label, and following a farewell gig at the
Lyceum in London, they split in March 1981. Many thought that Perrett
would pursue a solo career, or form a new band, but a lengthy fight
against drug problems kept his activities low key, and it was not until the
early 1990s that would finally make an active return with new material.
Perhaps appropriately, in 1992 a reissue of 'Another Girl, Another Planet'
finally registered modest success in the UK singles chart.

Recommended CD listening: 'The Immortal Story' (Columbia 471267-2)

Sex Pistols' God Save The Queen.
It won't be on the new album and it may not be
out at all for very long.
So get it while you can.
Sex Pistols' God Save The Queen.
Available only as a single from Saturday May 28th
at shops with the sign.

Virgin Records V

PUNK!

THE PARTISANS

Somewhat short-lived in terms of their record career, the Partisans were a teenage punk band from Bridgend, South Wales, formed at the time of the second punk explosion in 1981. The quartet were very strongly influenced by The Sex Pistols, despite the raucous Oi! scene in which they developed (they played on the 'Oi Against Racism And political Extremism But Still Against The System' package tour, with Blitz and other bands). After a track appeared on Secret's 'Carry On Oi!' compilation album in October 1981, their tight, driving sound attracted the punk indie label No Future, to which they became the second signings. The anti-authoritarian 'Police Story' was their debut single early in 1982, followed a few months later by '17 Years Of Hell', a three-track single which also included the pointedly-titled 'Bastards In Blue'. After this, they quickly faded from view as the mohicaned wave of punk retreated from the headlines to the sidelines, though it's unlikely that any of The Partisans found alternative employment in the police force!

Recommended CD listening: 'Police Story' (Anagram CDPUNK 4)

PENETRATION

North-East England's most significant contribution to the late-1970s punk scene, Penetration (named after the Iggy Pop song of that title) were formed in the late Summer of 1976 in Ferryhill, County Durham, after 18-year-old former art student Pauline Murray and her friend Robert Blamire had seen The Sex Pistols play in Manchester. The original line-up was Murray (vocals), Blamire (bass), Gary Chaplin (guitar) and Gary Smallman (drums). They made their live debut at the Rock Garden, Middlesborough in October 1976, and after playing their first London gig in the following January (at the Roxy club, supporting Generation X), were invited to record some demos for Virgin, eventually signing towards the end of the year, when 'Don't Dictate' became their debut single, setting a style of strident, passionate and sometimes visionary lyrics which would become the band's on-stage and on-record trademark. There was a hiccup at the beginning of 1978, when Chaplin, the main songwriter up to this point, tired of gigging pressure and quit. He was eventually replaced by two guitarists: first a friend of the band, Neale Floyd, who settled down as rhythm player, and in mid-1978, the more metallic-inclined Fred Purser, who gave the band an altogether heavier sound. Their 1978 singles 'Firing Squad' and 'Life's A Gamble' got good reviews but no chart action, though the LP debut 'Moving Targets' reached a healthy No.22 in October.

1979 was a year of heavy touring, both in Britain and the US, where the band became exhausted by long, arduous treks. The second album 'Coming Up For Air' was recorded by a heavily pressured band starting to suffer internal disharmony over musical directions, but nonetheless again found positive reviews, and charted satisfactorily at No.36 exactly a year

after its predecessor. By the time it appeared on the market, however, the band had already decided to split, with Murray in particular disillusioned with the way music business pressures had ridden roughshod over what she had considered an innocent, idealistic musical venture. The break-up was announced on home turf at a Newcastle City Hall gig – which was recorded and issued as a posthumous 'official bootleg' album.

A few months later, Murray and Blamire linked up with producer Martin Hannett, and with session players, recorded as Pauline Murray & The Invisible Girls, initially with some success – their single 'Dream Sequences' reached the Top 75, and the eponymous album made No.25. A live band was put together, but lasted only a short while due to further uncertainty about musical direction. Murray would continue to record through the 1980s, but only in a low-key independent fashion.

Recommended CD listening: 'Moving Targets' (Virgin CDV 2109)

PETER & THE TEST TUBE BABIES

Formed in Brighton, Peter & The Test Tube Babies first surfaced in 1978 with a track titled 'Elvis Is Dead' on the local Attrix label's 'Vaultage '78' various artists compilation of south coast punk contenders. From that start, however, the quartet comprising Chris Marchant, Nicholas Loizides, Peter Bywaters and Derek Greening had a lengthy wait (despite steady gigging recognition) until the Oi! phenomenon caught hold in 1981, to find themselves with two typically nihilistic tracks, 'Intensive Care' and 'Rob A Bank (Wanna)' on the EMI compilation 'Oi! The Album'. This led to a coveted Radio 1 John Peel session, and a deal with No Future for their first single, 'Banned From The Pubs', followed by 'Run Like Hell' and the live album 'Pissed And Proud', whose track listing read like a yobbo lifestyle guide ('Up Yer Bum', 'Keep Britain Untidy'), and which, like the two singles, was a major indie chart hit.

The band developed a penchant for manic label-hopping through the mid-80s, and assorted albums like 'The Mating Sounds Of South American Frogs' and 'Another Loud, Noisy, Blaring Punk Rock LP', and singles like 'Keys To The City', 'Zombie Creeping Flesh' and 'Rotting In The Fart Sack' (an EP) were spread across such outlets as Hairy Pie, Jungle and Trapper (the latter operated by the band themselves).

Compilations and reissues excepted, things went quiet for them on record after the 1986 album 'Soberphobia', but despite never crossing to mainstream chart success, the band were always popular stalwarts of the punk gigging circuit both in the UK and Europe, and continued their good-humoured stage yobbery even into the 1990s with no apparent loss of their core audience.

Recommended CD listening: 'The Best Of Peter & The Test Tube Babies' (Dojo DOJOCD 57)

The Poison Girls

PLASTIC BERTRAND

Belgium's major contribution to punk was Plastic Bertrand's international novelty hit 'Ca Plane Pour Moi', which reached No.8 in the UK in 1978, and was proclaimed by its originators as a "punque smash internationale". The artist's real name was Roger Jouret, formerly the drummer with a band named Hubble Bubble, who specialised in wacky versions of oldies. His Plastic Bertrand character came out of Two Man Sound, a comedy act involving Jouret and producer Lou Deprijck. 'Ca Plane Pour Moi' was a Continental hit at the end of 1977, and the subsequent UK release retainied its French lyric – almost entirely slang phrases, which emerged as gibberish when translated literally – on the British release. This proved no barrier at all to radio play, although there was some confusion over what exactly the title meant: BBC radio interpreted it as 'That's Alright By Me', while Bertrand unwisely sought to advise them that it was actually 'I'm High Because Of That'.

Staggeringly, Plastic Bertrand wasn't even just a one-hit wonder. He put together an album in the wake of the Top 10 single, which contained a ludicrous French-language version of the Small Faces oldie 'Sha La La La Lee'. Extracted as the follow-up single, it reached No.39 in the UK, and spent five weeks on the chart, before the phenomenon of Belgium's punk piss-taker was finally laid to rest.

POISON GIRLS

None of them were 'girls' as such: the band's lead singer Vi Subversa was a feminist and anarchist approaching middle age, while cohorts Richard Famous (guitar), Bernhardt Rebours (bass) and Lance D'Boil (drums) were all distinctly of the male persuasion. Formed in 1977, they first appeared on record in May 1979 with 'Closed Shop' and 'Piano Lessons' on a Small Wonder EP shared with the Fatal Microbes (whose guitarist Pete Fender was Subversa's son). The 12-inch min-album 'Hex' followed, containing eight abrasive cuts, and then in 1980 the band became involved with the similarly anarchistic Crass, for whose 'Bloody Revolution' 45 they provided the B-side 'Persons Unknown'. The Crass label also released the first Poison Girls album, 'Chappaquidick Bridge', in 1980, plus a further single, 'All Systems Go'. These all did well on the indie charts, and the band for a while had a higher profile, at least on the alternative market, than any other outfit whose recordings were so wilfully anti-commercial, abrasive and generally unsettling.

By 1981, the band had returned to their own Xntrix label, to release the live album 'Total Exposure', but were now suffering an audience decline for the idealistic anarcho-punk approach in the face of the more yobbish anti-establishment rant of the Oi! bands. They recorded briefly in 1983 for Illuminated Records (ever an early-80s home for arty impenetrables) without the public really noticing, then fell back on their own label devices once again for the 1984 album 'Seven Year Scratch' and feminist-stance single ('I'm Not A) Real Woman'. Neither was particularly well accepted, and the band cut one final set, released in 1985 as the wryly-titled 'Songs Of Praise', before finally splitting during that year.

Recommended CD listening: 'Real Woman' (Cooking Vinyl COOK CD 086)

The Police

THE POLICE

The Police's career as one of the most popular and successful bands in the world during the 1980s is a familiar tale full of multi-million-selling records, but in the context of the present book it should be noted that, as in the cases of Elvis Costello, Talking Heads and others, their proximity in the punk scene at the kick-start of their career helped define their sound, their image and even their musical direction. Notwithstanding guitarist Andy Summers' playing history with several 60s and 70s icons, the new sound The Police generated when Summers, Sting and Stewart Copeland hit their joint stride, was as much an energetic backlash against mid-70s dinosaur extravagance as that of The Sex Pistols or The Clash – in fact, it was more minimalist, and certainly owed far more to the rhythms and dub ambience of reggae (an influence which virtually all early punk bands attempted to absorb) – than that of either band. The spiky blonde-haired image which fused the three players as a visual unit was also important – a deliberate move by mentor Miles Copeland – putting The Police clearly on the right side of the new wave/old wave dividing line, and was one that many image-desperate punk outfits would have died for: some artists, like Billy Idol, merely did the same job on themselves. For the most obvious punk influences in The Police's music as such, check out their first recording, 1977's 'Fall Out' on Copeland's Illegal label. The trio may well have become a world-class act anyway, without first being rocked in the punk cradle and having their live gig grounding on the UK punk circuit, but they wouldn't have been The Police.

Recommended early CD listening: 'Outlandos D'Amour' (A&M 393 753-2)

THE POP GROUP

Perhaps the most inappropriately-named band of all time, The Pop Group's music was about as diametrically opposed to the upbeat, lightweight, and commercial connotations of the words 'pop group' as it was possible to be. Formed in Bristol in mid-1977, and comprising Mark Stewart (vocals), Gareth Sager (guitar), John Waddington (guitar), Simon Underwood (bass) and Bruce Smith (drums), they produced intellectual, anarchistic punk-angst diatribes of the most determinedly intense and bleak kind, which may be one reason why it took them 18 months to get their first record deal (with Radar), which produced the single 'She Is Beyond Good And Evil' in March 1979 and the album 'Y' a month later. Neither sold well, and after almost sinking under financial problems (they held a 'Bankruptcy Benefit' for themselves, to raise sufficient funds to continue), the band moved to Rough Trade, where their records began to score in the indie charts – the bitter 'We Are All Prostitutes' made the top 10, and the album 'For How Much Longer Must We Tolerate Mass Murder' (perhaps the most brutally negative rock album ever made) actually reached No.1 for three weeks in 1980. A couple of releases further on, though, the band split, with the members going off in significantly different musical directions – Sagar formed the dizzy jazz-funkers Rip, Rig And Panic, while Underwood went similarly lightweight and funky with Pigbag.

PUNK!

PRAG VEC

Comprising Susan Gogan on vocals, John Studholme on guitar, David Boyd on bass and Nick Cash on drums, Prag VEC formed in London in February 1978, following the demise of Gogan and Studholme's previous R&B band the Derelicts. They debuted on vinyl during December with the four-track EP 'Existential', on their own Rough Trade-marketed Spec label, and followed up in July 1979 with 'Expert', which they promoted on a ten-day UK tour shared (turns were taken at topping the bill) with two other left wing-orientated bands from the Rough Trade stable, Manicured Noise and the Monochrome Set. After this, the band cut an album, eventually released during 1981 as 'No Cowboys', again on Spec. This had quite elaborate packaging, including a free poster and badge, but so obscure was the release that hardly anybody found it. Overtaken by the noisier new wave of punk, the band dropped out of sight soon afterwards.

PROTEX

Formed by four school-leavers in Belfast early in 1978, Protex comprised David McMaster (vocals & guitar), Aidan Murtagh (vocals & Guitar), Paul Maxwell (bass) and Owen McFadden (drums) – all Clash fans who dreamed of emulating their idols, and became huge live favourites in Northern Ireland with a zippy punk/power-pop act. Like most young Belfast bands of the time, they gravitated to Terri Hooley's locally-based Good Vibrations label, which released their debut single 'Don't Ring Me Up' in November 1978. This was licensed in England by Rough Trade, and it gained sufficiently wide notice to result in the band signing to Polydor, on which major label they released three further singles – 'I Can't Cope', 'I Can Only Dream' and 'A Place In Your Heart' – plus the (later very obscure) album 'Strange Obsessions', during 1979 and '80. None of these records, however, sold in any significant quantity, and Protex were dropped by Polydor later in 1980, with comparatively little notice being taken of their subsequent split.

PUBLIC IMAGE LTD.

Producing music which has never had very much connection with punk save the fact that the unmistakable tones of John Lydon, AKA Johnny Rotten, were delivering the vocals, Public Image Ltd (known almost from the beginning as PiL) are significant in the punk context in being arguably the first major post-punk band whose music was conceived with reference to the punk sound and ethos (unlike that of the new romantic and electronic bands), but worked hard at being its antithesis. Whereas punk, as typified by The Sex Pistols, was, despite its often angry or nihilistic subject matter, generally uplifting in terms of its fire, energy and liberated DIY simplicity, that of PiL was often menacingly dense, brooding rather than energetic, and manifested anger in a white noise sort of way rather than kicking ill-temperedly loose in a way that Eddie Cochran might have understood.

A lot of this had to do with the way Lydon was left angry and frustrated by The Pistols experience which had created his Johnny Rotten alter ego, screwed his life around for a couple of years, then spat him out when he threatened to kick against the traces. PiL was announced to the world in May 1978, when the remaining Sex Pistols were busy concocting nonsense with great train robber Ronnie Biggs; in October, they emerged with their first single 'Public Image', followed in December by the debut album of the same title. Lydon was concerned to make sure he was seen to be doing just what his previous public would not expect and couldn't cope with, and the original band was put together to deliberately fuse disparate influences: guitarist Keith Levene was classically-trained (though had played with The Clash early on), bassist Jah Wobble was immersed in reggae and dub, and drummer Jim Walker came from Canadian rock band The Furies. In the event, interest was such that both discs charted (the single reaching the top 10), and PiL would, ironically, eventually have a far longer recording career than The Sex Pistols, despite the fact that the band shed and gained (and sometimes regained) members at a rate of knots, broke up for long periods, and always strenuously tried to stay out of fashion. By the end of the 80s, PiL's charted albums would almost run to double figures, spinning off an even larger number of hit singles (including a top 5 smash, 'This Is Not A Love Song', in 1983). Lydon seemed to find his peace with the idea of the band (if not always its line-up) fairly early on, and had commercial acumen enough to return to it whenever he found new music coming on. Since it was all, in the first place, a product of his hatred for The Sex Pistols, PiL might be considered the illegitimate-child-made-good of punk.
Recommended CD listening: 'Public Image Ltd.' (Greatest Hits So Far) (Virgin CDV 2644)

THE QUADS

From Birmingham, a city whose contribution to the punk explosion was remarkably small, bearing in mind its size, The Quads were formed in 1979, and as a live act, quickly came to the attention of the Second City's most notable established indie label, Big Bear Records. Run by blues fan Jim Simpson, Big Bear mainly specialised in blues and R&B acts, but a brief diversion into New Wave at this time also gave it the likes of The Gangsters and Mis-Spent Youth. The Quads had most success, however: their debut single 'There Must Be Thousands' got wide exposure and found its way into the national charts, albeit at a lowly No.66. They followed up with 'There's Never Ben A Night', 'UFO' and 'Gotta Getta Job', and also had two live recordings on the Big Bear compilation 'Brum Beat Live At The Barrel Organ' (alongside The Dangerous Girls, Dansette Damage et al), but none of these sold in chartable quantities. The band then drifted from the limelight in the latter part of 1980, before eventually splitting.

John Lydon, ne Rotten, of post-Pistols PiL

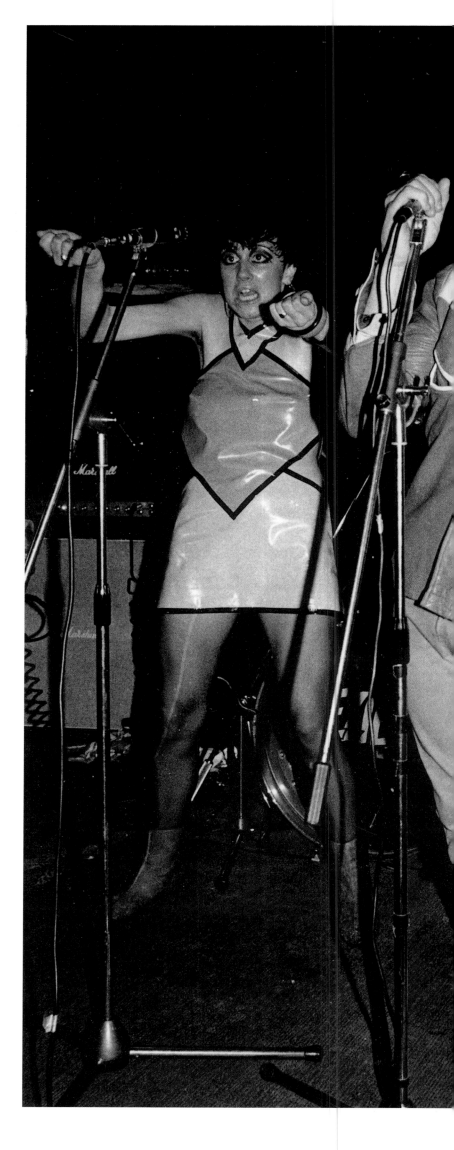

RADIATORS FROM SPACE

Signed by Chiswick Records' Ted Carroll in the Spring of 1977, The Radiators From Space actually came from Dublin, and had already been playing together for a couple of years, initially as Greta Garbage & The Trash Cans. The line-up was Steve Rapid (vocals), Philip Chevron (guitar), Peter Holidai (guitar), Mark Megaray (bass) and James Crash (drums). Their thundering debut single 'Television Screen' was Chiswick's first punk release, but the indie label didn't find the muscle to push it or the follow-up 'Enemies' chartwards, and Rapid decided to quit on the eve of the sessions for their debut album, leaving Chevron to take over lead vocal duties. Following the late-1977 release of the album, 'T.V. Tube Heart', the band began to gig solidly on the UK mainland, and early in 1978 shortened their name, for convenience, to The Radiators. They also began to work with veteran producer Tony Visconti, who produced several further singles and, in July 1979, a second album, 'Ghostown'. This tie-up, however, still failed to bring about a commercial breakthrough on record, which would always elude the band despite their gigging credentials. The quartet split in the early 80s, with Chevron resurfacing as producer of The Pogues' 'Dirty Old Town' in 1985, and subsequently joining that band on guitar in time for their successes of the late 1980s.

Recommended CD listening: 'Ghostown' (Big Beat CDWIK 85)

THE RAINCOATS

One of the few all-girl punk groups to aspire to more than novelty value in the genre, The Raincoats were less commercially successful than either The Mo-Dettes or The Slits, but arguably had a more enduring influence on other musicians (for instance Nirvana's Curt Cobain, who was to publicly acknowledged it). Formed late in 1978, their original line-up comprised Ana Da Silva (vocals and guitar), Vicky Aspinall (guitar and violin), Gina Birch (bass) and the former Slits drummer Palmolive, who only stayed for the first 12 months. Throughout most of the band's subsequent career on record, a flexible pool of additional players (like drummers Richard Gudanski and Charles Hayward) would augment the core line-up, while their non-playing manager Shirley O'Loughlin was also counted as a full band member.

Rough Trade signed them early in 1979, and their debut single was the critically-rated 'Fairytale In The Supermarket' that April, with the album 'The Raincoats' – an encapsulation of their feminist-stance stage act, with some musical nods to their admitted Velvet Underground influence plus a highly original revival of the Kinks' 'Lola' – following in November. Following this at lengthy intervals was the more sophisticated (and guest player-heavy) 'Odyshape' in June 1981, and the eventual swansong release 'Moving' in January 1984, with a cassette-only issue, 'The Kitchen Tapes', on the US Roir label in 1983, giving an additional insight into the band's roots and essence. By the mid-80s, however, they had disbanded, leaving behind a strong blueprint for female self-determinism in rock which was still being recognised a decade later.

Recommended CD listening: 'The Raincoats' (Rough Trade R 3022)

PUNK!

Rezillos
Fay Fife and
Eugene Reynolds

THE REZILLOS & REVILLOS

The Rezillos came together at Edinburgh Art College in March 1976, in a large line-up which used the D.I.Y. ethos of punk to pursue a shared love of stomping 60s pop, R&B and glam-rock. The original players were vocalists Fay Fife and Eugene Reynolds, guitarists Luke Warm (Jo Callis) and Hi-Fi Harris, bassist D.K. Smythe, saxophonist William Mysterious, drummer Angel Patterson, and Gale Warning on backing vocals. They first gigged (in sparkly Thunderbirds/comic book stage costumes) around Scotland in November 1977, and in mid-1978 released their debut single 'I Can't Stand My Baby' for new indie label Sensible Records, which set them up for a major deal with Sire in November. At this point, Harris, Smyth and Warning all departed, and the remaining quintet relocated to London, with Mysterious now on bass. Despite much gigging support, the first Sire single '(My Baby Does) Good Sculptures' didn't chart, but the label sent the band to New York early in 1978 to cut their debut album, only to then sit on the completed recording for nearly three months while it organised a new UK distribution deal with WEA, leaving the band in financial dire straits while they waited to tour in support. Mysterious walked at this point, to be replaced on bass by Simon Templar, but the band then briefly tasted the big time when the album 'Can't Stand The Rezillos' hit No.16 in the charts and the second single 'Top Of The Pops' made No.17. A national tour with label-mates The Undertones in support also saw the follow-up 'Destination Venus' into the top 50, but by Christmas they had decided to split, with vocalists Reynolds and Fife going one way, and the instrumentalists the other. Their December 23 farewell gig at Glasgow Apollo was recorded and issued the following April as the live album 'Mission Accomplished …But The Beat Goes On', making No.30.

Callis, Templar and Paterson joined with Troy Tate (ex-Index) to form Shake, which played for 18 months with only moderate success. Reynolds and Fife, meanwhile, reunited with ex-Rezillo and recruited drummer Rocky Rhythm to form new band The Revillos, who were rounded out by three girl back-up vocalists. Signed by Virgin's Dindisc subsidiary, they made several singles, plus the album 'Rev Up', but only charted briefly with 'Motorbike Beat' in February 1980. Subsequent releases were on their own Superville outlet, but again the album 'Attack', plus assorted singles like 'She's Fallen In Love With The Monster Man' were not big sellers. The band's major problem was the instability of its personnel: Fife, Reynolds and Rhythm remained constant, but otherwise guitarists, bass players and (particularly) backup singers came and went in seemingly endless procession. Eventually, after self-financing a major American tour (undertaken by van!) and being let down over a mooted Sci-Fi music movie deal, The Revillos decided enough was enough, and quit.

Recommended CD listening: 'Can't Stand The Rezillos: The (almost) Complete Rezillos' (Sire 9 26942-2)

Cover art for 'Fairytale In The Supermarket' by The Raincoats

RAMONES

Formed in Forest Hills, New York, in January 1974, The Ramones were for many the archetypal US punk band: uncompromisingly straightforward, minimalist, raucous, energetic, and unencumbered by musical complexities, while being visually streetwise and (to outward appearances) eschewing any pretensions – in fact, they played it downright dumb: a cartoonist's notion of punk-rockers. Even their trademark stage slogan, 'gabba gabba hey' sounded like it came straight out of a comic!

The original line-up was Johnny Ramone (real name John Cummings, guitar), Dee Dee Ramone (or Douglas Colvin, bass) and Joey Ramone (aka Jeff Hyman, drums). They made their stage debut at the Performance Studio on New York's East 23rd Street on March 30, 1974, thanks to Johnny's friendship with Tommy Erdelyi, a recording engineer who part-owned the venue. Keen at first to manage the band, within weeks Tommy had taken over on drums (with Joey switching to vocals), and had become Tommy Ramone. The practice of adopting the band's name as each member's stage surname was one which would stick with the band for some years, and enabled them to kid early interviewers that they were all, in fact, brothers born with the name Ramone.

In August 1974 the four-piece band began a residency at Manhattan's

CBGB's club, where they became renowned for their rapid-fire numbers lasting an average of less than two minutes apiece. In October of the next year, they were signed by Sire Records, and the following April, their debut album 'The Ramones' appeared – 14 songs lasting some 28 minutes in all, cut in equally rapid-fire sessions that lasted just two weeks and cost only $6,400. It just failed to reached the top 100 in the US.

In July 1976, the band made its UK debut at London's Roundhouse, alongside The Flamin' Groovies and The Stranglers. The minimalism of their performance, plus their street yob uniform of leather jackets and ripped jeans (an image already glimpsed on the album sleeve), were to have a fundamental effect on much of the early British punk audience – those who couldn't keep up with the travelling fashion circus of The Sex Pistols' entourage now had a street corner role model which (ostensibly) needed very little musical talent to emulate.

A second album, 'The Ramones Leave Home', arrived in the Spring of 1977, and immediately sold best in the UK, where it made No.45 as the band arrived for a full British tour. Released in its wake was the single 'Sheena Is A Punk Rocker', which made UK No.22 and US No.81, and was the first hit single to actually use the word 'punk' in its title. The band hit their first bit of controversy over a track originally included on 'Leave Home', titled 'Carbona Not Glue'. Since this concerned sniffing of the said

substance, their UK licencee was not prepared to release the album with this track intact. The dispute was overtaken though, by one with the makers of Carbona, whose product name had been used without permission, and the end result was that the track was dropped anyway.

'Swallow My Pride' provided a second UK Top 40 hit in the Summer, but The Ramones' projected UK tour with The Sex Pistols later in 1977 was aborted. Their third album 'Rocket To Russia' was released, however, and this time made the US Top 50 as well as the British chart.

In May 1978, Tommy left the band to return to studio production work (though to remain as their producer), and was replaced on drums by Marc Bell, formerly with Richard Hell's Voidoids. Once in, he was re-christened Marky Ramone. This new line-up produced the 'Road To Ruin' album, which reached No.32 in the UK in the Autumn, though stalled at 103 in the American charts. The next year saw the double live album 'It's Alive' (recorded in London), which made the UK Top 30, while the band also appeared in Roger Corman's teen-trash film *Rock'n'Roll High School*, and performed, among other numbers, the title track. Neither the soundtrack album or the title single were among their biggest sellers, but the project did introduce the band to legendary producer Phil Spector, who remixed their tracks from the movie.

Spector stayed on to produce the Ramones' 1980 album 'End Of The Century', a collaboration which the band later derided. Nevertheless it included their biggest hit single 'Baby I Love You' (originally cut by Spector with the Ronettes), which made No.6 in the UK. The album too sold well, making the Top 20 in Britain and No.44 in the US, and boosted by this they undertook another major UK tour during the late summer of 1980.

Liaisons with unlikely producers then became a Ramones norm for a while, and inevitably their two-minute-spurt trademark began to further dilute in the process – though the inevitable '1-2-3-4' count-ins and general cartoon fun were still the hallmarks of their stage performances. Graham Gouldman of 10cc produced 1981's 'Pleasant Dreams' album, and Ritchie Cordell (of Tommy James & The Shondells fame) handled 1983's 'Subterranean Jungle'. Both were only moderate sellers on either side of the Atlantic, and The Ramones generally dropped out of critical reckoning, at least as far as their once-inviolate punk credentials were concerned. There was also another change of drummer during 1983, with Marky being replaced by Richard Beau from The Velveteens (who became Richie Ramone), while the band almost permanently lost Joey after he was rushed to hospital following a fight over a girlfriend, and had to undergo brain surgery to remove blood clots.

The band would continue to record an average of an album a year throughout the 1980s and even into the '90s (their mid-1995 set 'Adios Amigos' was ostensibly their farewell offering), though the zestful power-pop style they developed during the '80s (and which kept them moderately commercial) largely took them beyond the focus of the present book – despite some excellent recorded moments like the wry anti-Reagan swipe 'Bonzo Goes To Bitburg' in 1985. Later personnel switches would see the return of Marky in 1982, and the departure of Dee Dee in 1989 to become rap artist Dee Dee King (he was replaced on bass by C.J. Ramone). Both Joey and Johnny would also undertake the occasional solo project in the later years.

Recommended CD listening: 'Ramones Mania' (Sire 925709-2)

RICH KIDS

After bassist Glen Matlock was elbowed from The Sex Pistols in February 1977 for being too pop-orientated, he immediately began to put a band together which would better reflect his own rock'n'roll vision. First recruits, in March, were guitarist Steve New, who had rehearsed with The Pistols a year before, and drummer Rusty Egan. After some tentative gigs as a trio, they persuaded Midge Ure, at the end of his tether fronting Scottish pop group Slik, to throw in his lot as vocalist and guitarist, and with the mix complete, the band was swiftly signed by EMI. Both Matlock's and Ure's pop sensibilities ensured that The Rich Kids' music was going to be more sophisticated than a straight punk thrash, and they became early exponents of what was subsequently termed power pop. With Mick Ronson producing, their first sessions at the end of 1977 delivered the single 'Rich Kids', which climbed to No.24 the following February. Two more singles during 1978 failed to make the grade, but the album 'Ghosts Of Princes In Towers', released in October, reached No.51. However, by the time the LP was released, internal dissention and general disillusionment – partly caused by snide critical reaction to their post-punk stance – had already set in. The quartet agreed to split during the week their album charted, but kept quiet about it, individually sorting out career moves, until contractual obligations were fulfilled. Egan and Ure got Visage underway before the end of the year, while within six months Ure would be hit-bound with Ultravox. Both New and Matlock would later work with Iggy Pop.

Recommended CD listening: 'Ghosts Of Princes In Towers' (Dojo CD 151)

TOM ROBINSON BAND

Tom Robinson's music both pre-dated and outlasted punk, but he belonged to that band of visionary new-wavers (alongside Ian Dury and Elvis Costello) whose career was swept up and advanced by their time and place compatibility with the idiom. The original Tom Robinson Band was formed in November 1976, after Robinson left the acoustic outfit Cafe Society, but its six-piece line-up proved unstable and short-lived. A smaller, tighter outfit rose from the ashes in January 1977, comprising Robinson on bass and vocals, Danny Kustow (guitar), Mark Ambler (keyboards) and Dolphin Taylor (drums), and with a desire (inspired by The Pistols and The Stranglers) to make snappy, high-energy music. After six months of constant gigging and honing a fund of Robinson's own songs, the band were signed by EMI, and instantly scored a Top 10 hit with the stomping '2-4-6-8 Motorway'. In its wake came the anthem-filled album 'Power In The Darkness', which reached No.4, and the live EP 'Rising Free', which reached No.18 early in 1978 on the strength of the track 'Glad To Be Gay', in which Robinson proclaimed the empowerment of his homosexuality. 'Up Against The Wall' provided a third Top 40 single, before the band personnel began to change as first Ambler and then Taylor departed, being succeeded by several new keyboard players and drummers as the band

struggled to regain its original integrity. 'TRB 2', a second album in the Spring of 1979, reached No.18, but suffered a critical mauling for being musically dull and sloganeering, while the band's hit singles also dried up after 'Bully For You' crawled to No.68 in March. By the Summer of '79, Robinson found himself in a band with only one of the original members – himself – in it, and decided to break the outfit up. Six months later he would return with Sector 27 (deliberately leaving his own name out of that of the band this time), but eventually found more commercial success in the mid-1980s with a more mainstream solo style – particularly on the 1983 Top 5 hit 'War Baby'.

Recommended CD listening: 'The Collection, 1977-87' (EMI CDP 7 48543 2)

ROUGH TRADE

Rough Trade was a vital ingredient in the UK recording revolution which grew up around punk, initially as an independent record shop specialising in indie and new wave releases, and then as an independent label in its own right, and the hub of a distribution network for small labels which enabled them to bypass the machinations of the majors. Mastermind behind the operation was Geoff Travis, who opened the original shop, near Notting Hill Gate in London, in February 1976 – just at the time that the first indipendent labels were emerging and theearliest punk bands were being signed. Wholesaling of small labels began as outside demand for their releases grew, and Rough Trade would eventually grow into a key link in the national indie distribution network known as 'The Cartel', handling a number of important labels that included Mute, Factory, Postcard and Les Disques Du Crepescule.

The Rough Trade record label itself was launched at the beginning of 1978 with a Metal Urbain single, and it went on to sign Cabaret Voltaire, Stiff Little Fingers, Kleenex, The Raincoats, The Pop Group, The Monochrome Set, Essential Logic, Swell Maps, The Slits, Spizzenergi and The Fall, to name but a few, during the punk era. Many of the acts were nurtured by Rough Trade for a successful single or two before an inevitable poaching by a major, but with its ear so close to the street with regard to new and innovative talent, the label would regularly be able to replace a defected act with something equally arresting. Rough Trade had the first indie chart No.1 single with Spizzenergi's 'Where's Captain Kirk?' in January 1980, and No.1 indie albums from The Pop Group and The Fall during the same year.

Rough Trade's most successful home-grown act came in the post-punk years in the form of The Smiths, who remained with the label throughout their hitmaking career. After some tough financial periods during a couple of recessions (including the collapse of the distribution network in 1991), the organisation has survived – albeit in a slimmed-down fashion to suit the often leaner times – right up to the present day.

P<small>UNK!</small>

The Ruts

THE ROXY

Located at 41, Neal Street in Covent Garden, the Roxy Club (formerly a gay hangout) was, from the latter end of 1976, London's first dedicated live punk venue, and for the first four months of 1977 it accordingly became the genre's best-known live showcase in the city, presenting most of the new bands who were then poised to make it big, like The Clash, Buzzcocks, Adverts, X-Ray Spex and Siouxsie & The Banshees. The EMI Harvest label made a number of live recordings at the club during the early months of 1977, and the compilation album 'Live At The Roxy' (featuring most of the above plus Eater, Wire, Unwanted, Johnny Moped and Slaughter & The Dogs) was released at the end of April – ironically, just after the venue finally shut its doors following a farewell night headlined by Siouxsie & The Banshees.

THE RUTS

The Ruts came together in Southall, South London in August 1977, spurred by a shared love of the live punk experience – singer Malcom Owen, Guitarist Paul Fox and bassist Dave Ruffy were all audience regulars at the Vortex club. Initially lacking a drummer, they co-opted Paul Mattock, ex-Hit And Run, for early rehearsals, but by the time they began to gig regularly at colleges and the occasional Rock Against Racism event, Ruffy had switched to drums, John 'Seggs' Jennings was playing bass, and the band's style had settled into an individual reggae-punk blend . The self-styled

'Musicians' Collective' indielabel People Unite signed them in July 1978, and their debut single 'In A Rut' appeared the following January, immediately attracting the attention of Virgin, which promptly bought their contract, and BBC Radio, which gave the band a John Peel session in May 1979. On the heels of this came the Virgin debut 'Babylon's Burning', quickly hauling them into the punk aristocracy when it smashed to No.7 nationally in July, also giving impetus to the follow-up 'Something That I Said' (which reached No.29) and their brass-augmented and untypically polished debut album 'The Crack' (which hit No.16).

Curiously, the next single 'Dub War' failed to chart, but 'Staring At The Rude Boys' brought them back into the top 30 in May 1980. However, shortly afterwards, on July 14, Owen – who had earlier written the song 'H-Eyes' as a warning message against hard drugs – was found dead of an accidental heroin overdose. This seemed likely to end the band, but the others elected to continue, with new keyboards-playing member Gary Barnacle, as the slightly re-named Ruts DC (from the Latin 'da capo', or once more from the beginning). Their album 'Grin And Bear It', and single 'West One (Shine On Me)' were both hits later in 1980, but new material lacked the cutting vocal and songwriting edge which Owen had provided, and as they looked for a less rock-orientated rhythmic reggae direction on subsequent albums 'Animal Now' and 'Rhythm Collision Vol.1', their basic appeal slipped away, and little more was heard of the band.

Recommended CD listening: 'You've Gotta Get Out Of It' (Virgin COMCD 7)

THE ROXY
LONDON WC2
(Jan - Apr 77)

mjbbfsjbcpiuswdbfv;sdjkh
jhv wdoujhvg vefcouhg kjwv
fouyg ofuyGoGHvcfovbv
foYG hbwcmjbbf-
sjbcpiuswdbfv;sdjkh jhv
wdoujhvg vefcouhg kjwv
fouyg ofuyGoGHvcfovbv
foYG hbwcmjbbf-
sjbcpiuswdbfv;sdjkh jhv
wdoujhvg vefcouhg kjwv
fouyg ofuyGoGHvcfovbv
foYG hbwcmjbbf-
sjbcpiuswdbfv;sdjkh jhv
wdoujhvg vefcouhg kjwv
fouyg ofuyGoGHvcfovbv
foYG hbwcmjbbf-
sjbcpiuswdbfv;sdjkh jhv
wdoujhvg vefcouhg kjwv
fouyg ofuyGoGHvcfovbv
foYG hbwcmjbbf-
sjbcpiuswdbfv;sdjkh jhv
wdoujhvg vefcouhg kjwv
fouyg ofuyGoGHvcfovbv
foYG hbwcmjbbf-

sjbcpiuswdbfv;sdjkh jhv
wdoujhvg vefcouhg kjwv
fouyg ofuyGoGHvcfovbv
foYG hbwcmjbbf-
sjbcpiuswdbfv;smjbbf-
sjbcpiuswdbfv;sdjkh jhv
wdoujhvg vefcouhg kjwv
fouyg ofuyGoGHvcfovbv
foYG hbwcmjbbf-
sjbcpiuswdbfv;sdjkh jhv
wdoujhvg vefcouhg kjwv
fouyg ofuyGoGHvcfovbv
foYG hbwcmjbbf-
sjbcpiuswdbfv;sdjkh jhv
wdoujhvg vefcouhg kjwv
fouyg ofuyGoGHvcfovbv
foYG hbwcmjbbf-
sjbcpiuswdbfv;sdjkh jhv
wdoujhvg vefcouhg kjwv
fouyg ofuyGoGHvcfovbv
foYG hbwcmjbbf-
sjbcpiuswdbfv;sdjkh jhv
wdoujhv kjwv fouyg
ofuyGoGHvcfovbv foYG
hbwwdoujhvg vefcouhg
kjwv fouyg
ofuyGoGHvcfovbv foYG
hbwc

PUNK!

Contrary to popular belief, The Sex Pistols did not simply originate as a gleam in Malcolm McLaren's entrepreneurial eye. Certainly, McLaren would be the chief architect of what they became — which was the single most important punk act of all; the genre's focal Beatles or Elvis equivalent which everyone else either imitated, reflected or tried to better — but if the band itself is traceable back to a glint in anybody's eye, it would have to be that of Steve Jones.

In 1972, would-be guitarist Jones was a (largely truant) schoolboy and active petty thief. Much of his time which should have been spent at school, was actually passed at the nearby home of his friend Warwick Nightingale, along with another absconder, Paul Cook. Nightingale first had the idea that they should try to put a band together, since he already played guitar. For a while, Jones systematically stole various instruments and items of equipment to equip them, including part of a drum kit (which Cook completed by buying the rest on HP). Cook initially decided to be the vocalist, along the lines of his hero Rod Stewart, although he didn't have much of a voice. At the time, two other schoolmates, Jimmy Mackin and Steve Hayes, completed the line-up, on organ and bass respectively. Tentatively, they decided to call themselves The Strand, after the Roxy Music track 'Do The Strand'.

Jones would often hang out at Malcolm McLaren and Vivienne Westwood's 50s gear shop Let It Rock in the Kings Road at weekends, usually on the lookout for an opportunity to steal something. He knew McLaren had some customers with connections in the music business , and from the early part of 1973, when The Strand were more or less together and playing, Jones began to try interesting McLaren in them, and pestered him into helping the band find a decent rehearsal location. Probably to shut Jones up, McLaren found a suitable room in Covent Garden Community Centre, though when he went to hear them play, was not overly impressed, particularly as they were by now without a bass player.

The shop also solved that problem, however. One of its Saturday helpers was Glen Matlock, an art student who, McLaren learned, also played guitar. Before long, he had introduced Matlock to the others and persuaded him to switch to bass, and by mid-1994 the band finally had a stable rehearsing line-up of Jones, Nightingale, Matlock and Cook. Towards the end of the year, leaving his friend Bernie Rhodes to oversee what the band were doing, McLaren went to New York, mostly to continue his ongoing fascination with The New York Dolls. He gave The Dolls an image make-over and became their unofficial manager over the winter, but then found himself presiding over their break-up. He returned to London in May 1975, having tried to persuade both former New York Doll Sylvain Sylvain and Richard Hell of Television to go with him and front the new band he had on the boil in Britain. Both turned down the prospect, though, and McLaren returned to Britain alone. However he did bring back a guitar belonging to Sylvain, which he somewhat symbolically (though even he probably didn't think so at the time) gave to Jones.

Frustrated by his failure to import an American, McLaren was still sure that if the band were to mean anything, they needed a new frontman-cum-vocalist, and that Jones should shift to what he was beginning to do much better — just play guitar. Jones himself went along with this, and perhaps surprisingly, the band as a whole (the victim excepted) had no compunction

about a re-shuffle which involved the ejection of founder member Nightingale — a much more withdrawn character than the others, he didn't really fit the design which McLaren was starting to sketch in his head.

After a couple of months in which *NME* writer Nick Kent was tried out as vocalist/guitarist, McLaren's eye alighted on John Lydon, a green-haired(!) teenager with an abundance of attitude and image-consciousness, offset by a nervous shyness, who regularly hung out with his friends in the Kings Road shop (which by now was re-named Sex). At the end of August 1995, a suspicious Lydon was auditioned as a vocalist by being cajoled into singing along to a couple of Alice Cooper singles on the jukebox at Sex. The other three disliked him at first sight, but nonetheless it was clear that he was the right singer for them, and so the new quartet began rehearsing in earnest. Around the same time, McLaren also settled an ongoing quest for a new band name by bestowing 'Sex Pistols', a phrase/slogan which had cropped up on one of Sex's controversial T-shirts. (He had in mind the band's potential as a performing advertisement for the shop, and claimed he wanted to sell 'lots of trouser' off them). The band also found a new name for Lydon: on the basis of Jones constantly baiting him over how rotten his teeth were, he became colloquially known as Johnny Rotten, and the name stuck.

The band worked on a mixture of songs, including several Small Faces numbers, 60s garage and R&B hits like 'Psychotic Reaction', 'Watch Your Step' and 'Don't Gimme No Lip, Child', and some proto-compositions of their own, such as 'Submission', 'I Did You No Wrong' and 'Pretty Vacant'. On November 6, 1975, they finally ventured out for their first gig, playing a support slot to Bazooka Joe at St. Martin's School Of Art in London's Charing Cross Road. Only five songs were played before they had the power pulled on them, but their ragged noise sufficiently impressed a couple of audience members to get them a second booking the very next night at Central London Polytechnic. Scattered dates followed through the next month or so, but a key one was at Ravensbourne Art College at Bromley in Kent, where almost the only interested audience member was a mesmerised Simon Barker, who quickly spread the word about this outrageously offbeat band to his friends, setting the 'Bromley Contingent' of ardent Sex Pistols camp followers into motion. Eschewing normal booking procedures, McLaren had the notion of the band turning up at college gigs by other acts, and brazening it on to the stage by claiming to be the official support act. Though these gigs brought in no money, they were a valuable part of the stage learning cycle, and the tactic worked more often than not. McLaren was also determined to keep the band off the traditional London pub band circuit, which in his mind would simply add them to the interchangeable menu of pub-rockers who were a signigicant part of the mid-70s scene; it was important that The Pistols stand out as something original in their own right, and to the same end he also encouraged the dropping of most 60s and R&B covers from the stage act, and a concentration on the material the band themselves were producing, however fragmentary some of these songs might have been.

The band gigged steadily, spreading outside the London area for the first time (as far afield as Manchester, Sheffield and Middlesborough), through the first half of 1976. They picked up fans and detractors in more or less equal amounts, with music press coverage similarly divided between

the excited and the sneering. Outbreaks of violence were not unknown at gigs – probably an inevitable result of the extreme reactions The Pistols generated – and Dingwalls in London actually banned them from future appearances, which was a taste of things to come. Another ban came in August when the organisers of the Mont De Marsan Punk Festival in France refused to have The Pistols on the bill because a reputation for trouble had preceded them (The Clash, who *were* invited, then withdrew in solidarity). They did, however, play the 100 Club Punk Festival in London at the end of September, alongside the prototypical Siouxsie & the Banshees who included, on that occasion, Sid Vicious playing drums. This event too was marred by violence (in which Vicious was implicated, but not The Pistols), causing the 100 Club to ban punk bands thereafter. Perhaps of more importance for the band themselves at this time was that EMI A&R man Nick Mobbs viewed several gigs during the week or so after the festival, and decided to sign them. In the midst of competing interest from Polydor, Chrysalis and Mickie Most's RAK label, the EMI deal was signed on October 8, accompanied by the payment of half of a £40,000 advance. The debut single 'Anarchy In The UK' was recorded nine days later, with producer Chris Thomas at the controls.

On December 1, five days after the single's release, The Pistols caused their biggest media splash yet when EMI's promotional team ill-advisedly booked them as a late replacement for Queen on Thames TV's early evening magazine programme *Today*. An interview with presenter Bill Grundy rapidly descended into taunts and four-letter ripostes, causing the national press the following morning to explode with 'punk shocktroopers from hell are in our midst'-type headlines. McLaren could not have created a wider-reaching or more controversial publicity coup if he had carefully planned and executed it himself. Disaffected youth all over the country was suddenly aware of the nihilistic liberation inherent in punk, and it is quite possible that a fair number of the other bands covered in this book shook themselves into potential as a result of that single two-minute slanging match in a London TV studio.

Less amused by the furore was EMI. With 'Anarchy' only three weeks in the shops, and showing at No.38 on the singles chart just prior to Christmas, the company began to cave in to external pressures and internal misgivings. Firstly, the chairman offered an apology for the band's behaviour, and then, a week into the new year, announced that the company and the band had 'mutually agreed to terminate their recording contract', with EMI statiing that it felt 'unable to promote this group's records internationally in view of the adverse publicity'. The Pistols were paid off with the second half of their negotiated £40,000 advance.

While all this was ensuing, the 'Anarchy In The UK' national tour, which had been due to last through the whole of December 1976, was decimated by venue and local authority bans in the aftermath of the Bill Grundy fiasco and ensuing tabloid tirade. The Pistols managed to play only three of 19 scheduled dates (in Leeds, Manchester and Plymouth), plus a handful of hastily-arranged replacements. The tour lost McLaren and the band some £10,000, but the press coverage continued to spiral upwards.

The next upheaval came in February 1977, when Matlock left the band after several months of elevating personality clashes (particularly between him and Rotten) and differences of musical opinion (between Matlock and all the others). The Pistols claim to have fired him, and he claimed to have told them he was quitting, but whichever was the case, McLaren was already grooming long-time camp follower Sid Vicious (real name John Ritchie) as a replacement bassist – a process which first involved Vicious learning how to play a bass guitar! Nevertheless, by the end of February, he was rehearsed and in the line-up – and in McLaren's view, with his wasted, menacing demeanour, a perfect additional visual complement to Johnny Rotten's nervous mania.

In March, The Pistols were signed to a new recording deal, this time with A&M Records. In the by now familiar style of PR lunacy surrounding the band, they were photgraphed signing the deal on a trestle table parked outside Buckingham Palace – an allusion to the fact that their first A&M release was to be a song titled 'God Save The Queen'. This time, McLaren was paid £50,000 for the band's services. However, in a surreal development that even he could not have predicted (or, presumably, engineered), he was back at A&M's offices five days later to receive an additional £25,000 as compensation payment – A&M had fired The Sex Pistols. The label was fairly tight-lipped about the reasons, but it seems that possible 'industrial blackmail' from other elements of the industry vital to A&M's existence, and a tide of resentment among its existing artist roster, had combined to cause second thoughts. McLaren publicly crowed about them touring record companies collecting cheques, and the publicity value was again immeasurable, but once again the band were left high and dry with no recording outlet. Despite being the highest-profile rock act in the land at the time, there was no music by them in the shops for anyone to buy.

The impasse was solved in May when, third time lucky, McLaren agreed a deal with Virgin (for a £15,000 advance) and the company did not back out of it! 'God Save The Queen' was released at the end of the month, and immediately, another almighty kerfuffle began. Since the single coincided with the national celebrations of Elizabeth II's Silver Jubilee, it was felt by many to be a pointed insult. The press attacked the sleeve design (by Jamie Reid), which depicted the Queen's face with punk-style safety pin added, BBC Radio and most of the commercial network denied the song airplay on 'taste' grounds, certain large retail chains (notably W.H. Smith) refused to stock it in their shops, and the single almost failed to get manufactured at all, when workers at the pressing plant objected to it. It eventually made No.2 in the national chart during Jubilee week, below a Rod Stewart single – though it topped the *NME*'s chart, which took less data input from the large chains which were refusing to sell it. The Pistols celebrated Jubilee Day itself by having a riverboat party on the Thames. They performed 'Anarchy In The UK' live within across-the-water earshot of the Houses Of Parliament, and as a result had the police awaiting them with charges when the boat docked.

The second half of 1977 finally saw The Pistols delivering, and being rewarded, commercially, though inevitably there was still noshortage of controversy. The next single 'Pretty Vacant' (ironically, co-written by the departed Matlock) reached No.6 at the end of July, and the BBC didn't object to it, allowing the band to perform on *Top Of The Pops*. Following a short tour (most gigs being played under pseudonyms to avoid repetition of the previous December's bans), 'Holidays In The Sun' then went to No.8. In November, the long-awaited Sex Pistols album, 'Never Mind The Bollocks – Here's The Sex Pistols', was released and immediately topped the LP chart, although it took a minor court case to confirm that it was not actually an offence for shops to display an album sleeve with the word 'bollocks' on it

to public gaze! The rock press, meanwhile, carped that a high proportion of the tracks on the album were the band's already-released singles, though in fact it did fully encapsulate the pick of the repertoire which the group performed in their live stage act.

On Christmas Day, 1997, the band played what would prove to be their final gig, when they gave an imprompu charity performance to an audience of pre-teens. Come the new year, they flew to the US (after overcoming a last-minute visa ban) to undertake what was designed as the tour to break them in America. Instead, it broke the band up. The Pistols played a couple of US TV slots, and gigs in Atlanta, Memphis, San Antonio, Baton Rouge, Dallas, Tulsa and San Francisco, where their performance at the Winterland Ballroom saw the band on stage together for the last time. Several of the gigs were marked by audience violence, and by the end of the 'Frisco show the band had had enough of the tour, the audiences, Amercia, McLaren, each other, and – basically – The Sex Pistols. On February 17, Rotten said he was quitting and McLaren said that he was fired anyway. Vicious made his point in typical fashion by overdosing and getting himself hospitalised. Cook and Jones, still an inseparable duo despite everything, decided to go to Rio, pursuing a whim to meet fugitive Great Train Robber Ronnie Biggs. McLaren returned to London, pondering what he could salvage from the mess.

Rotten/Lydon, of course, would never return to the fold. Staying with Virgin as a recording artist, he would form Public Image Ltd. later in 1978. The other three remained Sex Pistols, at least in name, and had another UK Top 10 hit in July with a single coupling 'No One Is Innocent' (a track which Cook and Jones had recorded with a vocal cameo by Ronnie Biggs) and Vicious' Z-movie version of the Frank Sinatra standard 'My Way'. After this, Vicious effectively ceased to function as a band member, and after playing a 'Sid Sods Off' farewell gig in London with back-up from various punk alumni, he moved to New York with his American girlfriend Nancy

Spungen. In October, Spungen would be found stabbed to death in the couple's New York hotel room, and Vicious was arrested for her murder and jailed. McLaren bailed him with money from Virgin, but Vicious was on an unstoppable path to self-destruction, and on February 2, 1979, still out on bail awaiting trial in the US, died from a heroin overdose.

McLaren determined to have the Pistols saga close with a bang rather than a whimper by completing production on the Julien Temple-directed film *The Great Rock'n'Roll Swindle* (his re-drawing of what The Pistols had been about all along). During 1979, the band's financial affairs were taken to court for resolution (though it would take until 1986 before everything was settled and the principals would get what was owing to them). The movie was released in October, and with supreme irony, music from it gave the deceased band (Cook and Jones had 'sodded off' too, to form a new outfit called the Professionals) a flurry of chart activity, with both their revivals of Eddie Cochran rockers 'Something Else' and 'C'mon Everybody' hitting the No.3 spot, the terminally stupid 'Silly Thing' making No.6, and the double album from the film reaching No.7. Even an LP of interviews and soundbites (including the Bill Grundy debacle) was able to hit No.6 in the chart. In a last mad rush, McLaren's dream of pointless trash smash success by the ultimate rebel band, piled up before him, in excess. Undoubtedly, he revelled in the irony, and fuel was certainly added to his assertion thereafter that the whole Sex Pistols 'situation' was a manufactured sham on his part. Whatever The Pistols were 'supposed' to represent, though, their very existence proved to be one of rock music's occasional twists on its axis, leaving it with a new direction to explore. Punk was the mid-70s' version of an occasionally necessary act – the kick up the backside of rock music complacency – and the Sex Pistols were the boys wearing the boots.

Recommended CD listening: 'Never Mind The Bollocks - Here's The Sex Pistols' (Virgin CDV 2086) and 'The Great Rock'n'Roll Swindle' (Virgin CDVD 2510)

PUNK!

The Saints

THE SAINTS

Formed in 1975 in Brisbane, Australia, The Saints were the first punk band from Down Under to make any international impact. Chris Bailey (vocals), Ed Kuepper (guitar), Kim Bradshaw (bass) and Ivor Hay (drums) first came to notice in the UK when their Australian single '(I'm) Stranded' was issued by the UK Power Exchange label at the end of 1976, and enthusiastically reviewed in the rock press. EMI's Harvest label offered the band a deal on the back of it, and they moved to London for the UK release of their debut LP 'The Saints' in February 1977. The second single to be taken from the album, 'This Perfect Day', charted at No.34 in July, and was followed by a wide-ranging UK tour, though the next single surprisingly went nowhere. A second album, 'Eternally Yours', was recorded in London towards the end of the year, with new bassist Alisdair Ward replacing Bradshaw, who left to join The Lurkers. The album was a moderate seller the following Spring, and the band immediately began working on a third set, which appeared in September as 'Prehistoric Sounds', and showed more of their pre-punk soul/R&B influences becoming prominent. The LP had only been on the market a couple of weeks, however, when the band announced that they were to split, citing a difficult relationship with their record company as their main frustration. Hay and Kuepper returned to Australia (where the

latter was to form The Laughing Clowns), while Bailey held on to The Saints' name, and with various accompanying musicians, would revive it quite frequently for new recordings during the 1980s, mostly for the French New Rose label. All the original players apart from Kuepper came back into the ranks at some point, but later versions of the band would never recapture the impact they had for a short while during punk's first heyday.

SCRITTI POLITTI

Formed at college in Leeds in 1978, and originally comprising Green Gartside (vocals), Nial Jinks (bass) and Tom Morley (drums), Scritti Politti were for a short period the epitome of DIY punkdom, with an explicit left wing political message (their name came from the book *Scritto's Republic*), only to transform themselves into smooth funksters once commercial success pointed a less painful course. They moved to Camden Town, London, in the latter part of the year, and started their own shoestring label operation St.Pancras Records, debuting with the single 'Skank Bloc Bologna', whose three tracks were illustrative of their cross-matching of jazz and reggae influences with punkish rock and sparse electronics.

PUNK!

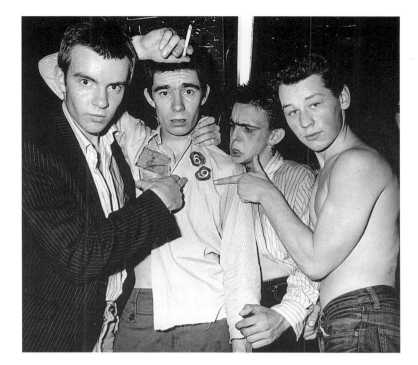

SHAM 69

Although surrounded by an East End image of working class solidarity, Sham 69 were put together in Hersham, Surrey, by Jimmy Pursey, initially a glam-rock follower who also happened to be an active class idealist, and who recognised the early strains of punk as being ideal for channeling his vociferous energy. The first Sham 69 comprised Pursey (vocals), Neil Harris (guitar), Johnny Godfornothing (guitar), Albie Slider (bass) and Billy Bostik (drums), but in June 1977, Pursey sent almost all of them packing because they failed to share his commitment to their songs. Bassist Slider initially remained, while in came guitarist Dave Parsons and drummer Mark Cain to launch a new, sleeker, 4-piece band, who made their first single, 'I Don't Wanna', a couple of months later for the indie Step Forward label. On the strength of this, they were signed to a major deal by Polydor in October, whereupon Slider left and Dave Treganna took over on bass, to complete the definitive Sham 69 line-up.

The first Polydor single, in January 1978, was the archetypal rabble-rousing 'Borstal Breakout', which didn't chart, followed by the band's debut album 'Tell Us The Truth', which made No.25. After this, the hit singles arrived in earnest: 'Angels With Dirty Faces' reached No.19, and then the stomping, anthemic 'If The Kids Are United' and the laddish 'Hurry Up Harry' were both top tenners before the end of the year. Their second album 'That's Life' closed 1978 peaking at 27.

Sham, however, had an increasingly rough ride at their live gigs. Much to Pursey's dismay, his rabble-rousing stage style, essentially a battle cry for working class self-assertion, tended to attract genuine rabble – skinheads looking for bovver, and worse still, right wing and racist yob activists out for still more malignant mischief. The band actually withdrew from some gigs where trouble was known to be promised in advance, but it seemed that almost any Sham 69 show was subject to a skinhead invasion before the end of the act. After a full-scale riot at a Hendon gig in January 1979, Pursey announced an end to the band's live work. They attempted isolated 'farewell' gigs during the first half of the year, but when a concert at London's Rainbow collapsed under fighting in 20 minutes, time was finally called, with Pursey considering plans to work with former Sex Pistols Steve Jones and Paul Cook. On record, ironically, they were still peaking in 1979: 'Questions And Answers' made No.18 in the Spring, while 'Hersham Boys' in August was the band's biggest-ever single, hitting No.6, and its parent LP 'The Adventures Of The Hersham Boys' reached No.8 a month later. They were persuaded back to some live activity to promote the latter (with a new drummer, Rick Goldstein), but by now the press was attacking Sham's credibility too, and they were clearly on a hiding to nowhere. The final line-up kept it up until the Summer of 1980, when Pursey went one way as a soloist (he got a new deal with Polydor which quickly foundered on non-success), and the others joined ex-Dead Boys vocalist Stiv Bators as The Wanderers.

Pursey would have a fitful solo career in the early 1980s, including another fruitless recording deal with Epic, though he clearly found more job satisfaction producing records for others. Eventually, in the early 90s, with punk nostalgia now in full swing, he would put together a new line-up of Sham 69 to play the revival circuit.

In 1979, the band teamed St.Pancras with Rough Trade Records, and this guaranteed a wider distribution of their work. The EP '4 A-Sides' in November won them a session slot on John Peel's Radio 1 show, and soon after these tracks too were duly pressed on vinyl as the 'Peel Sessions' EP. Both records sold well enough to make it onto the UK's new indie chart early in 1980.

Jinks left the band in 1980, and it was the end of the following year before fortune finally smiled on them as the jazzy ballad 'The Sweetest Girl', released on Rough Trade, went to No.64 in the charts. Then in 1982 came 'Faithless' and the double A-side 'Asylums In Jerusalem'/'Jacques Derrida', each of which sold progressively better. Still more successful was the album 'Songs To Remember', which made No.12 in September 1982. After this, the mainstream beckoned, as Scritti Politti (which by now for all intents and purposes meant Green, with accompanying musicians as required) were signed to Virgin Records and went on to have ten hit singles and two more Top 10 hit albums over the next decade. This hitmaking incarnation, needless to say, was a very long way from the minimalist stance of their overtly punk beginnings.

Recommended CD listening: 'Songs To Remember' (RoughTrade ROUGHCD20)

Recommended CD listening: 'The First, The Best And The Last' (Polydor 513

SIOUXSIE
& THE BANSHEES

Susan Dallion, known as Suzy or Siouxsie to her friends, first came to notice on the punk scene as one of the Bromley-based fans who followed The Sex Pistols around the London club circuit in 1976. At the time, her outrageously experimental modes of dress were an integral part of the 'Bromley Contingent''s notoriety, as well as being a seminal influence on the punk fashion boom in general.

On September 20, 1976, during the opening night of the 100 Club Punk Festival, Souixsie took her initial step from camp follower to performer when she and some friends got together a spontaneous performance group in order to secure their own spot in the festival between The Subway Sect and The Clash. Accompanied by a hasty assemblage of Marco Pirroni (guitar), Steve Havoc (bass) and Sid Vicious (drums), with a name inspired by a recent TV screening of the Vincent Price horror movie *Cry Of The Banshee*, Siouxsie performed (as opposed to sang) an open-ended medley of The Lord's Prayer aided and abetted by 'Twist And Shout' and bits of 'Knocking On Heaven's Door'. The quartet kept it up for 20 minutes before abruptly stopping – because they'd got fed up before the audience apparently had (the crowd, by all accounts, had been stunned by the sheer audacity of what was going on...)

A few weeks later, Siouxsie formed a new version of the band, this time not as a one-off, but to rehearse as a proper performing unit. Havoc (later Steve Severin), decided to learn his bass properly and stay on, while Peter Fenton joined on guitar, and Kenny Morris came in on drums. This line-up eventually debuted live as support to The Heartbreakers at Croydon's Red Deer in February 1977, playing Marc Bolan's '20th Century Boy' along-side half-a-dozen original songs. Similar gigs followed through the spring, and the band cut some demos for Track Records in June (to no positive result), until in July Fenton left and was replaced on guitar by John McKay, who was, infact, a former fan.

The major mystery throughout the latter half of 1977 was why no record label paid any attention at all to the now regularly gigging

Banshees, despite the fact that arguably less popular punk outfits were being signed all around them. They almost put out the fruits of their November John Peel Radio 1 broadcast on a self-distributed EP, until the idea was scotched by BBC red tape. Eventually, after rejections by EMI, Chrysalis, Decca, Anchor and other labels which had already signed punk contemporaries, the band finally, in June 1978, got a favourable deal with Polydor. They undoubtedly savoured the moment when, three months after this, their debut single 'Hong Kong Garden' soared into the chart and peaked at No.7: several bands signed months earlier were still struggling for any kind of a hit at the time.

The band made their first headlining UK tour in the Autumn, before releasing their debut album 'The Scream', which drew positive reviews, and charted at No.12 just before Christmas. On stage, Siouxsie developed a striking, always instantly recognisable image, carrying over elements of her Bromley Contingent days, while pulling the focus to her strikingly made-up eyes and face. Her wailing, untrained, yet ever more controlled vocals, counterpointed by the Banshees' stark punk thrash, ensured the outfit's popularity at a time when some of the earlier punk bands were already starting to run out of on-stage steam.

Three hit singles followed in 1979: 'The Staircase (Mystery)' (No.24), 'Playground Twist' (No.28), and the strange, teutonic 'Mittageisen (Metal Postcard)' (No.47), while a second album, 'Join Hands', reached No.13 in the early Autumn. However, shortly after the album's release, the band was suddenly plunged into crisis when, on September 7, McKay and Morris abruptly decamped prior to a gig in Aberdeen. The music papers were full of 'Banshees split!' headlines, but in fact within 10 days not only was the band back on the rails, but the tour recommenced too. Budgie, former drummer with The Slits, came in to fill Morris' stool, while Robert Smith of The Cure (who were The Banshees' support band) offered to double up in the short term as Siouxsie's lead guitarist as well as that of his own band. As if all this were not enough, though, at the end of October Siouxsie collapsed on stage at Hammersmith Odeon, and was diagnosed in as having hepatitis. Ordered to take a two-month rest from touring, she was forced to cancel The Banshees' remaining commitments.

Budgie was confirmed as the band's permanent drummer at the end of 1979, while early in 1980, John McGeoch of Magazine was recruited as guitarist – at first on a 'help out' basis, and then full-time from the middle of the year. The band scored a third Top 10 album in 1980 with 'Kaleidoscope', and more hit singles with 'Happy House', 'Christine' and the Christmas-orientated 'Israel'. They also toured the US for the first time before the end of the year.

1981 delivered another Top 10 album in 'Juju' (spinning off the No.22 hit single 'Spellgound'), and also a retrospective singles compilation titled 'Once Upon A Time', which made No.21 at Christmas. Otherwise, the year was memorable for the fact that Siouxsie and Budgie also indulged themselves in a spin-off recording project as The Creatures: their single 'Mad-Eyed Screamers' made No.24.

During a mid-1982 Scandinavian tour, Siouxsie contracted laryngitis, and was advised the rest her voice for 12 months. Nevertheless, a new album, 'A Kiss In The Dreamhouse', was recorded in the Autumn, and charted at No.11 in November. McGeoch was ill prior to the UK dates designed to promote the album, so Robert Smith stepped in to play guitar on stage once more - he ended up staying until May 1984, after McGeoch decided to leave during his own absence. Smith and Severin worked together on their own spin-off project the Glove at this time, to counterpoint further Creatures activity by Siouxsie and Budgie which resulted in the album 'Feast' and the hit singles 'Miss The Girl' No.21) and 'Right Now' (No.14). The Banshees as such took a back seat through most of 1983, but came back in a bang in October with a commercial-sounding revival of

The Beatles' 'Dear Prudence', which proved to be their biggest-ever single in the UK, reaching No.3. It was followed by a live double album, 'Noctune', and then in mid-1984 by 'Hyena', which hit No.15. Smith departed back to full-time work with The Cure just prior to this album's release, with John Carruthers (formerly of Clock DVA) coming in on guitar.

The band would keep on an equally successful path through the second half of the 1980s and into the 90s, having outlived the punk phenomenon which – even more so than many other bands – had truly created them out of nothing. The increasing sophistication of their music from the early 80s onwards put them on a completely different level to any of the surviving exponents of punk: they possibly indulged themselves in music closer to their roots when "moonlighting" as The Creatures. There would be a period of successfully reviving oldies: new versions of Dylan's 'This Wheel's On Fire' and Iggy Pop's 'The Passenger' would both make the chart in 1987. Amazingly, the band would also start to sell records in major quantities in America from the late '80s onwards, with one latter-day single - 1991's 'Kiss Them For Me' - actually climbing higher in the US (No.23) than in the UK (No.32). Such transatlantic success would eventually see Siouxsie & The Banshees featuring on the 1991 'Lollapalooza' tour of alternative rock acts, alongside such latter-day punks as The Butthole Surfers, Jane's Addiction and Nine-Inch Nails: punk finally coming around full circle, one generation down the line.

Recommended CD listening: 'The Scream' (Polydor 839008-2) and 'Once Upon A Time: The Singles' (Polydor 831 542-2)

THE SKIDS

One of Scotland's major contributions to the original punk scene, The Skids, comprising Richard Jobson (vocals), Stuart Adamson (guitar and vocals), Willie Simpson (bass) and Tom Kellichan (drums) formed in Dunfirmline in 1977. Their initial recordings comprised the 'Charles' EP, released by No' Bad Records, an indie label formed on their behalf by local record shop owner (and early manager) Sandy Muir. This brought them to the attention of Virgin, which signed the band in May 1978, with minor hit singles following in 'Sweet Suburbia' and the EP 'Wide Open', led by 'The Saints Are Coming'.

The band hit top gear early in 1979 with the racing, anthemic 'Into The Valley', which made the Top 10. Their debut album 'Scared To Dance', full of similar guitar-driven anthems, went to No.19, despite being the result of sessions which saw major disagreements between guitarist Adamson and producer David Batchelor. Adamson considered quitting the band, but eventually relented for another two years. In the meantime, two more Top 20 hits with 'Masquerade' and 'Working For The Yankee Dollar', plus a Top 40 success with 'Charade', were the successful extracts from the next album 'Days In Europa', recorded with ex-Be Bop Deluxe guitarist Bill Nelson in the producer's chair (and on keyboards), which reached No.32. Just after its release, Kellichan left the band, and the Rich Kids' Rusty Egan sat in for him briefly before a permanent replacement was found in Mike Baillie. Next to go was Simpson, who was replaced by Russell Webb. Then, after recording the third album 'The Absolute Game', which soared to an impressive No.9 and spun off the minor hit singles 'Circus Games' and 'Goodbye Civilian', Adamson finally quit in June 1981, fired with the vision of a new guitar-led band which would emerge the next year as Big Country. Baillie also went at around the same time, leaving The Skids as Jobson and Webb, who worked on the final album 'Joy' with session help. By this time, Richard Jobson was already actively pursuing his other interests of acting and writing, appearing in a somewhat controversial London stage production and publishing the poetry collection *A Man For All Seasons*. When 'Joy' failed to sell in any significant numbers, and his other stage commitments also meant musical activity became prohibitive, Jobson made the decision to end the band early in 1982. He worked for a while in 1984 with Webb and others in a band called The Armoury Show, which produced one album, 'Waiting For The Floods', but his longer-term career ambitions in the fields of broadcasting, acting and writing ensured that this project would be short-lived.

Recommended CD listening: 'Dunfirmline' (Virgin COMCD 10)

SLAUGHTER & THE DOGS

From Wythenshawe in South Manchester, where the band members had attended Sharston High School, Slaughter & The Dogs got together at the beginning of 1976, playing around Greater Manchester pubs with an act that combined David Bowie glam influences with an MC5-like punk rant, and invariably involved the scattering of large amounts of talcum powder for a 'smoky' stage effect. The original line-up consisted of Wayne Barrett (vocals), Mike Rossi (guitar), Howard 'Zip' Bates (bass), and Eric 'The Mad Muffett' Grantham (drums). A little over a year after their first gigs, in the wake of the appearance of a couple of late-76 live tracks on the 'Live At The Roxy' compilation, they became the first act on new Manchester indie label Rabid, which released their debut single 'Cranked Up Really High' in May 1977. This in turn brought them to the attention of Decca, to which they were among the very first new wave signings. However, three Decca singles over six-months, including an aggressive revival of the bubblegum oldie 'Quick Joey Small', failed to sell, and by mid-1978, disillusionment had set in, leading to the announcement of a split just days before Decca released their first album, 'Do It Dog Style'.

The break-up proved even more disillusioning, however. Despite Decca dropping their contract, several of the band decided to get back into good form for live gigging before the end of the year. Rossi and Bates were still on board, and they recruited new drummer Phil Rowland (formerly with Eater), guitarist Billy Duffy, and – briefly – Duffy's friend Steve Morrissey as vocalist. Morrissey departed, depressed, after the band failed a recording audition, and Rossi took over the vocal duties. Eventually, they returned to vinyl again in May 1979 with the EP 'It's Alright', which emerged on Manchester's TJM label, but the release was almost universally overlooked, and in a radical move, the quartet changed their name to Studio Sweethearts, signing to DJM Records. After one single, it became clear that this venture was a hiding to nowhere, and amazing, yet another version of Slaughter & The Dogs then re-emerged, with the original four members! They had more gigging luck than The Studio Sweethearts, but no greater success on record, despite a few releases on DJM. Ed Banger replaced Barrett on vocals in the latter days, but the band faded from view during the second onslaught of Oi!/punk. Short-term members Duffy and Morrissey later proved to have far more success elsewhere of course, with The Cult and The Smiths respectively.

Cut

the slits

THE SLITS

With members drawn from the original punk fan scene which grew up in London around The Sex Pistols and the other early UK punk bands, The Slits came to be probably the most influential female act in the genre, even though their commercial success was not particularly spectacular. They formed in January 1977, when Viv Albertine (guitar) and Palm Olive (drums), both of whom had rehearsed with Sid Vicious' didn't-quite-make-it band The Flowers Of Romance, joined with guitarist Kate Korus and Suzy Gutsy, recruiting a 14-year-old friend named Arianna Forster (who soon shortened her name to Ari Up) to handle the vocals. Gutsy and Korus departed quickly (the latter to form The Mo-Dettes), and Tessa Pollitt came in on bass guitar in time for the four-girl line-up to make their stage debut supporting The Clash at Harlesden during March. Despite a rough-and-ready stage approach quite appropriate for a group still learning their instrumental technique, The Slits had energy and punk attitude aplenty, and were then invited by The Clash as support on the White Riot tour.

The others eased out Palm Olive in October 1978, but were unable to find another suitable girl drummer, so with another Clash support tour in the offing, they recruited a male, Budgie, who had been in Liverpool bands The Spitfire Boys and Big In Japan.

After two years of being ignored by record companies, The Slits were signed to a one-album deal with Island in April 1979. The album, 'Cut', was made with the reggae producer Dennis Bovell, a teaming which produced an arresting punk/dub combination, as well as emphasising the tribal-style rhythms which had become a Slits stage trademark (and which in a later era would have aligned them with 'world music'). Released in the September, the album reached a creditable No.30 in the chart, and spun off a double A-side single coupling 'Typical Girls' and the group's revival of Marvin Gaye's 'I Heard It Through The Grapevine', which crept to No.60. Their version of the latter was already familiar as the theme to BBC Television's *Grapevine* programme.

Budgie, who had drummed on the LP sessions, had already left in July 1979 (to resurface in Siouxsie & The Banshees). The band then struggled to make their identity felt on record, as two singles for Y/Rough Trade and one for the tiny Human label in 1980, made only minimal impact. The next year, they signed to CBS, and with the assistance of Pop Group drummer Bruce Smith, made a second album, 'Return Of The Giant Slits', but lacking the confrontational energy which had characterised the early Slits, this failed to sell. At the beginning of 1982, the girls decided that enough was enough, and split up.

Recommended CD listening: 'Cut' (Island IMCD 90)

PATTI SMITH

Although obsessed with rock music, from Little Richard to Bob Dylan to The Rolling Stones, since childhood, Patti Smith did not actually become a rock performer until her late 20s, and then came at it obliquely through rock journalism and writing poetry, heavily inspired by Rimbaud and Burroughs. Living in New York at the beginning of the 1970s, she published three anthologies of poems – *Seventh Heaven, Kodak* and *Witt* – between 1971 and 1973, The latter year saw her doing public poetry readings at the Mercer Arts Centre, and at an event known as Rocking Rimbaud at Les Jardins in November that year, she performed at a well-received reading accompanied by rock critic Lenny Kaye, who played guitar. Her friend and manager Jane Friedman, on the back of this success, persuaded Smith to try singing rather than just reading her poetry to accompaniment, and in March 1974, the first Patti Smith Group came into being, with the vocalist backed by Kaye's guitar and the piano of Richard Sohl. A single, coupling her own (semi-autobiographical) 'Piss Factory' with the rock standard 'Hey Joe', was released on the Mer label (an enterprise by Kaye and artist Robert Mapplethorpe) in August, By now, Smith's reputation as a performer was burgeoning, and her group were regular favourites at CBGB's and other influential Manhattan clubs.

Early in 1975, Czech-born guitarist Ivan Kral swelled the ranks of the group and their sound, and he was followed shortly afterwards by the drummer J. D, Daugherty. A few months later, Smith was signed to Arista, and a debut album, 'Horses', was released in the Autumn. Produced by John Cale, it collected widespread rave reviews, and climbed to No.47 in the American LP chart.

1976 saw two UK and European visits, the second trek in the Autumn coinciding with the release of the second album 'Radio Ethiopia' — which got a lukewarm critical reception and sold less well, peaking at US No.122. To cap this disappointment, during a concert in Tampa, Florida, in January 1977, Smith took a 14-foot tumble offstage, her injuries forcing her into a neck brace and off the road for a lengthy recuperation period. She returned to changes, and by the time of her recovery in the Autumn, Sohl had left the group, and Bruce Brody (formerly with John Cale) joined on keyboards, in time to play on the Jimmy Iovine-produced third album 'Easter'. Released the following Spring, this, by far the strongest integration of Smith's lyrics with a solid rock accompaniment, was to be her biggest commercial success. A Top 20 album on both sides of the Atlantic, it also contained the dramatic power-rocker 'Because The Night', co-penned by Smith and Bruce Springsteen, which became a smash single, hitting No.13 in the US and No.5 in Britain.

Such big-time success was however, comparatively short-lived. The 1979 album 'Wave', produced by Todd Rundgren, was also a Top 20 US seller (No.41 in the UK), but faded from view much more quickly, and its featured single 'Frederick' only just grazed the charts. After she married Fred 'Sonic' Smith, the former MC5 guitarist, in March 1980, Smith shut down her performing career in favour of domesticity, and would not return to recording until 1988, when she resurrected some of the old vocal and lyric fire on a comeback album, 'Dream Of Life'.

Recommended CD listening: 'Easter' (Arista 251 128)

SPIZZ ENERGI

The mercurial Spizz, who never told anyone his real name, made his stage debut ranting frantically as a solo vocalist at Birmingham Barbarella's punk festival in August 1977. Two months later, he teamed with guitarist Pete Petrol (nee O'Dowd) to form Spizz 77. On the basis that this sounded out of date as soon as 1978 came along, the duo metamorphosed into Spizz Oil, thereby inaugurating a trend whereby if a name was worth keeping for longer than about two minutes, it just wasn't good enough for Spizz. As Spizz Oil, the duo made two singles, '6,000 Crazy' and 'Cold City', for Rough Trade, before, during 1979, Petrol departed and Spizz linked with new musicians Pete Hyde (guitar), Jim Solar (bass), Mark Coalfield (keyboards) and Hero Shima (drums), to become Spizz Energi. This line-up assured their permanent footnote in rock history by, early in 1980, being the first act to top the UK's newly-established indie chart – for an impressive seven weeks – with their offbeat single 'Where's Captain Kirk?', which had originally been released more than six months earlier. At this point, A&M stepped in with a major label deal, only to find that Spizz Energi were already no more: the band which A&M signed were Athletico Spizz 80. Their single 'No Room'/'Spock's Missing' was a good seller, but the first album 'Do A Runner' did exactly that from the sort of success that A&M had been hoping for.

And so it went on. As each new year arrived, Spizz changed his band's name again, and the 80s saw The Spizzles, Spizzenergi 2, Spizzorbit, Spizzsexual, Spizzivision, and even plain old Spizz, all of whom contrived to remain always on the cult fringes of the rock scene. Enough musicians came and went to crew a small battleship, with original guitarist Petrol returning and leaving with such seeming regularity, it seemed like Spizz had him on a particularly long piece of elastic. Eventually, Petrol became a computer programmer and then emigrated to New Zealand, finally severing the partnership, but Spizz would still be found occasionally gigging (normally under his best-remembered name, Spizz Energi) in the same old crazed punk style in the 1990s.

STIFF LITTLE FINGERS

Stiff Little Fingers (named after a Vibrators song) came together in Belfast in May 1977, the initial line-up comprising Jake Burns (vocals and guitar), Henry Cluney (rhythm guitar), Ali McMordie (bass) and Brian Faloon (drums). Unlike their local contemporaries The Undertones, whose upbeat music was essentially escapist, they concentrated (at the urging of journalist and co-writer Gordon Ogilvie, who became their manager) on material which focused on youthful life in Troubles-torn Northern Ireland, as exemplified in their debut single 'Suspect Device', released on their own Rigid Digits label in March 1978. Interest in this on the UK mainland prompted a move to London in September, at which point a hoped-for deal with Island fell through, but they toured with The Tom Robinson Band and did a John Peel Radio 1 session, and Rough Trade agreed to be the band's distributor, releasing the follow-up single 'Alternative Ulster'. Early in 1979, after an unexpected drumstool replacement of Faloon by Jimmy Reilly, Rough Trade released the band's debut album 'Inflammable Material', which, supported by Peel and others in the media, made history as the first album from the indie label sector to reach the UK Top 20 – it peaked at No.14, and stayed a spectacular 19 weeks in the chart, selling over 80,000 copies.

After another well-received indie single, 'Gotta Get Away', the band were signed by Chrysalis in August 1979, in a deal which gave their Rigid Digits production company full creative control. The first Chrysalis single, 'Straw Dogs', made No.44 in October, heralding the album 'Nobody's Heroes', which streaked to No.9 the following Spring, and spun off 'On The Edge', which was their biggest hit single, making No.15. Following extensive UK, European and US touring, they then released the live album 'Hanx' in September, gaining another Top 10 hit.

1981 produced the album 'Go For It!', which made No.14, plus the minor hit singles 'Just Fade Away' and 'Silver Lining', after which Reilly left the group, and was replaced by Dolphin Taylor, former drummer with The Tom Robinson Band.

By 1982, the band, despite a high profile and strong public following, seemed to be fighting a rearguard action against leaving behind their urgent punk roots for the musical mainstream, and that Autumn's album 'Now Then' highlighted this struggle, having a much more obvious pop sensibility than the intense earlier material. Burns clearly felt a confusion of direction, and left early in 1983 to form The Big Wheel (and eventually join Radio 1 as a producer), after which Stiff Little Fingers simply crumbled away. Against the odds, though, they would eventually reform some seven years later, with former Jam bassist Bruce Foxton in place of McMordie.

Recommended CD listening: 'All The Best' (Chrysalis CDS 797741-2)

Punk!

STIFF RECORDS

Launched in July 1976 by Dave Robinson and Jake Riviera, with the help of a £400 loan from Riviera's friend Lee Brilleaux, the lead singer with Dr. Feelgood, Stiff was by no means Britain's first independent label (several such were active in the 1950s), nor even the first of the punk-era crop (Chiswick was already active when Stiff's first single appeared), but a clever talent for image promotion (via slogans, t-shirts and witty press ads), and equally smart marketing on shoestring budgets, helped it become the flagship of the UK indie record movement. Stiff, because it was highly visible and patently with it, was the inspiration for the avalanche of do-it-yourself labels which came along in the wake of punk and were the chief talent-breeding ground of new wave music generally.

In some ways, this was ironic, since Stiff was never a particularly punk-orientated label. Robinson and Riviera were prime movers in the London pub-rock movement of the mid-70s, and Stiff's first single, in August 1976, was by Brinsley Schwarz survivor Nick Lowe (who nonetheless became very involved in punk on the production side).

However, the label did make the first important punk signing – The Damned, in September 1976 – and released the first recognised British punk single when the same band's 'New Rose' beat The Sex Pistols' 'Anarchy In The UK' into the shops by a week or two in November.

However, Stiff never scored a hit single with The Damned, and dropped the band early in 1978 before they had made any commercial break through. The label's first chart success was Elvis Costello's 'Watching The Detectives', in the closing weeks of 1977 – following which, Riviera left the company, taking his management clients Costello and Lowe with him, to form Radar Records.

In 1978, Stiff hit a hot streak after a couple of false starts with Ian Dury, culminating in the No.1 hit 'Hit Me With Your Rhythm Stick' – a near million-seller – at the end of the year. More big hits followed from Lene Lovich, Jona Lewie and Devo (whose early material Stiff licensed from the band's own Booji Boy label). Other acts like Richard Hell, The Adverts, Wreckless Eric, The Yachts and The Members passed through the Stiff portals during the punk era, mostly pit-stops on their way to more success elsewhere. When the 80s came along, the label was to have a seemingly endless series of Top 10 hits with Madness, and it maintained its long-term commitment to having a crack with anything interestingly off-beat or downright weird – even Tenpole Tudor and The Plasmatics found commercial success with Stiff. The label will always be remembered, though, for being in the right place at the right time, and with the right attitude, when punk came along to turn British rock music upside down.

the stranglers

A band who both pre-dated and survived the punk movement, while immersing themselves fully in the genre at its height and yet always ploughed an individual (and often controversial) furrow in terms of agenda, attitude and song lyrics, The Stranglers also had a more consistent success rate than all but the biggest of their contemporaries.

The band first came together in Guildford, Surrey, during the latter half of 1994, and grew from the ashes of an outfit called Johnny Sox, which vocalist/guitarist Hugh Cornwell had originally formed while working in Sweden. This band lived and rehearsed above an off-licence owned by their recently-recruited drummer, Jet Black (Jeth Whitethorne), but fell apart when two American members decided to return home. The gap was partly filled by local acquaintance J.J. (Jean-Jacques) Burnel, a guitarist who opted to learn the bass in order to be part of the band, and the resulting trio began to play prolifically around the Surrey pub and club circuit, initially calling themselves The Guildford Stranglers. By early 1975, however, this had shortened itself in use to The Stranglers, and that was the name that subsequently stuck.

For a while, the band was a four-piece via the addition of the Swedish guitarist Hans Warmling, a former Johnny Sox member, but after he returned to Scandinavia, the others decided to further augment their sound by having a keyboards player as fourth member, and in July 1975, they recruited Dave Greenfield, an experienced musician from Brighton.

At the end of 1975, The Stranglers signed a management deal with Albion, a major London booking agency, and as a result found their way into the London pub circuit and then on to often exhausting club tours all over the country, travelling in a former ice cream van belonging to Black. Their stark, aggressive stage act was often seen as being intimidating by audiences (and they never compromised, whether the crowd yelled for more or walked out en masse). But with equally snotty and noisy punk bands starting to spring up everywhere as 1976 moved on, The Stranglers came to realise that a suitable musical environment had caught up with them, rather than the other way around.

After lengthy attempts by the management to get a record deal, the band were eventually signed in December 1976 by United Artists Records' Andrew Lauder, and put in the studio with producer Martin Rushent. Debut single '(Get A) Grip (On Yourself)' appeared in February and charted at No.44, only to have its progress sabotaged by an inadvertent error in the chart compilation system which allocated its sales to another single. Two months later, however, the album 'IV: Rattus Norvegicus' was released, and caused wide surprise (not least to the band themselves) by streaking to

these peaked around No.40). Inevitably, though, success was accompanied by a hard ride: a riot at a Portuguese gig very nearly hospitalised the band, and the aftermath left them with lingering bad PR in Europe after they were falsely accused of having beaten up the gig promoter in retribution.

Real disaster finally struck in the Spring of 1980, when Cornwell, found guilty of possession of heroin, cocaine and cannabis, lost his appeal against a jail sentence, and was locked up in Pentonville for five weeks. Perhaps surprisingly, though, the band's audience took this enforced absence from the stage apparently in their stride, and business resumed more or less as usual upon Cornwell's release – until the whole band were arrested in France a couple of months later, accused of inciting an audience riot in Nice. They avoided prison this time, but were found guilty and later fined.

March 1981 belatedly saw a new album, the enigmatic 'Meninblack', which revolved around the X-Files-like concept of a kind of extra-terrestrial hit squad. The Stranglers' music to be found on it was probably their most sinister and alienating yet, but all the same, it made No.8 in the chart. Singles released during the year were only moderate sellers, however, and it was not until early in 1982 that the band finally scored another top 10 hit single. 'Golden Brown' was, in fact, their biggest-selling single ever (more than 600,000 copies), and reached No.2. Its wide appeal, thanks to a strong melody and an arresting waltz-time harpischord arrangement, showed how far from the punk-influenced early material The Stranglers' music had now changed – although the surreptitious revelation (some time later, by Burnel) that the oblique lyric was actually referring to heroin perhaps showed that the band could still be as anarchic as ever – merely more subtle about it. Nevertheless, 'Golden Brown' was also later to win a coveted Ivor Novello Award, as the 'Most performed work of 1982'. The hit single gave a major boost to its parent album 'La Folie', which reached No.11. The title track (sung by Burnel, entirely in French) was then a minor hit, before the Stranglers pulled off a further Top 10 single entry during the Summer of '82 with 'Strange Little Girl'. This was their swansong for EMI (which had absorbed United Artists along the way): in November the band signed a new long-term recording deal with the CBS' Epic label.

The Stranglers would continue performing and recording prolifically through the 1980s and into the next decade, having long since outlived any vestige of the punk scene which kick-started their hugely successful career. Like The Damned and Siouxsie and The Banshees, their very longevity has made them a mainstream musical institution where once they had been irritating punk rebels fighting the banning of their gigs. Moreover – and even more uniquely – the line-up would remain stable for more than 15 years, not changing until Hugh Cornwell, having developed a parallel solo recording career, finally departed in the Summer of 1990. Even then, The Stranglers would still carry on, with a new vocalist in Paul Roberts, and former Vibrator John Ellis joining on guitar. They look like being the only major name band from the Class of '76 which will be able to celebrate the twentieth anniversary of the punk explosion while not having to specially re-form for the purpose.

Recommended CD listening: 'The Singles (The UA Years)' (Liberty CDP 791 796-2) and 'The Old Testament: The UA Studio Recordings (1977-1982)'

No.4 – the first-ever punk top 5 album success. Successes, controversies and minor hitches then ensued – most of the latter in the form of cancelled gigs as various authorities around the country sought to ban 'undersirable' punk bands appearing in venues under their control. Growing success came on record, as three singles – the double A-side 'Peaches'/'Go Buddy Go', 'Something Better Change' and 'No More Heroes' all hit the Top 10 within five months of each other. The latter was also the title track of the Stranglers' second album, which made an impressive No.2 in October 1977. Any controversy generally concerned the band's song lyrics – 'Peaches' was banned by BBC radio for being 'offensive', and they also began to take some general critical stick over an alleged misogyny that seemed to characterise much of their material.

The band was at a commercial high point through 1978 and 1979, touring widely overseas (including the USA), recording three more charting albums – 'Black And White' (No.2), 'Live (X Cert)' (No.7) and 'The Raven' (No.4) – and adding to their Top 20 single score with 'Five Minutes', 'Nice'n'Sleazy', 'Walk On By' (a Doors-styled revival of the old Dionne Warwick hit), and 'Duchess'. It was not until the end of '79, with 'Nuclear Device' and 'Don't Bring Harry', that singles sales began to tail off (both of

Subway Sect

THE SUBURBAN STUDS

Formed in 1977 and hailing from Birmingham, this quartet were among the early rash of punk bands to gain a recording contract – with the Pogo label, which despite its punk-cred name and indie characteristics, was marketed by major conglomerate WEA Records. Their debut release was 'Questions'/'No Faith' in June 1977, but it didn't mean a lot, despite widespread gigging including a London stint at the Hope & Anchor which was captured on the Front Row Festival live compilation album taped at the venue. 'I Hate School' followed in March 1978, and two months later came the album 'Slam', which rounded up the singles, stage numbers like 'Bondage' and 'Throbbing Lust', and a revival of the Who's 'My Generation'. Sales were again quite minimal in the wake of what seemed like scant promotional support from Pogo, and the band joined the ranks of the great overlooked, disbanding in comparative obscurity before the end of the 1970s.

Recommended CD listening: 'Slam (The Complete Suburban Studs Punk Collection'(Anagram CDPUNK 21)

SUBWAY SECT

Formed in London in July 1976, and supposedly named after Hammersmith subway, where they played a couple of early rehearsal-type gigs, Subway Sect were an initially promising element of the first UK punk explosion for whom luck ran out early. Comprising Vic Godard (vocals), Robert Symmons (guitar), Paul Myers (bass) and Paul Packham (drums), they made their debut as part of the 100 Club Punk Festival on September 20, 1976. Packham only stayed aboard for three months before being replaced on drums by Mark Laff, but after the band had toured as support to The Clash on the latter's 'White Riot' trek, Laff too left (to join the newly-formed Generation X), and Rob Ward became the band's drummer.

After a UK tour in their own right, Subway Sect made their vinyl debut in March 1978 on Clash manager Bernie Rhodes' indie label Braik Records, with the single 'Nobody's Scared'. When it sank without trace though, Godard decided a personnel shuffle was in order, leading to the departure of Myers and Symmons. A new version of the band, comprising Godard, Ward, John Britain (guitar), Colin Scott (bass), and Steve Atkinson (keyboards), supported The Buzzcocks on their UK tour, and released a second single, 'Ambition', this time on Rough Trade. Again the record sold insignificantly, however, and the band ground to a halt during 1979 amid general apathy. Although Godard would revive the Subway Sect name a year or so later with a batch of new musicians, the original punk style of the band would be gone, with a weird blend of mock MOR/jazz in its place. Needless to say, this band wouldn't make it, either.

SWELL MAPS

Having first played together while still at school in the early 70s, the group of Solihull teenagers who would become Swell Maps got serious as a band in January 1976. Initially comprising Nikki Sudden (usually known as Nikki Mattress – vocals, guitar and piano), Biggles Books (guitar), Jowe Head (bass) and Epic Soundtracks (drums and vocals), they made a number of I recordings later in the same year, which did not see the light of vinyl until, early in 1978, the band established their own Rather Records label, in association with Rough Trade. A three-track single headed by 'Read About Seymour' was pressed up in a batch of just 2,000 copies, which Rough Trade had no problem shifting. By this time, guitarist Golden Cockrill and bassist/vocalist Phones B. Sportsman were also in the ranks for the now-legendary sloppy, jokey Swell Maps live gigs, although the band showed no apparent hurry to re-enter the studio (they also claimed to only rehearse about once every six months), because when a belated follow-up single appeared as late as March 1979, it was led by 'Dresden Style', recorded way back in 1976. However, by mid-1979, some three-and-a-half years of intermittent sessions had provided sufficient content for the truly weird LP 'A Trip To Marineville', whose 17 tracks (plus a free 4-track EP on early copies) ranged from perfunctory snippets to epic pieces, and from minimalist punk to serious piano works. Despite the oddities and contradictions, however, the album was another good seller in the indie field, and opened the way for the band's most commercial single, 'Let's Build A Car', which early in 1980, soared high into the upper reaches of the indie chart. This, however, seemed to be the last straw for the calculatedly disorganised Maps, who split up less than two months later, lest they should accidentally create a mainstream hit for themselves. Most of the members moved off into solo work, but the posthumously assembled second album 'Jane In Occupied Europe' served up another strong batch of reminders of their appealingly untogether togetherness.

Recommended CD listening:'A Trip To Marineville'(RoughTradeMAPS001 CD)

PUNK!

TALKING HEADS

Although, like Elvis Costello and The Police, their musical style could hardly ever be described as punk, Talking Heads (again like the aforementioned) needed the punk environment, with its new audience appreciation of the pared-down, the bleak and the challenging, in order to give a context to their oblique but infectious pop-funk. Had they emerged at the same time as The Eagles, America and The Carpenters, Talking Heads would simply have made no musical sense, but arriving on a New York scene which was already embracing The Ramones, Blondie and Television, their unorthodoxy and witty anti-romanticism were embraced by audiences – even though, like the punk outfits with whom they shared the CBGB's stage, they took some time to break through to commercial success.

The core of the band, Scottish-born David Byrne (vocals and guitar), Tina Weymouth (bass) and Chris Frantz (drums), had previously been part of a college band named The Artistics, at the Rhode Island School Of Design in Providence. When, after graduating, they relocated to New York City early in 1975, they got jobs by day, and rehearsed in their communal loft apartment by night, selecting for themselves the name Talking Heads out of TV guide. They made their live debut at CBGB's on June 20, 1975, supporting The Ramones, and eventually got a recording deal with Sire at the beginning of 1977, debuting with the quirky single 'Love Goes To Building On Fire'. At the same time, the fourth member, guitarist Jerry Harrison (formerly with Jonathan Richman's Modern Lovers) joined to make the band a quartet, and free Byrne to concentrate on vocals.

Talking Heads' most overtly punk-orientated period was through 1977 and 1978, notably demonstrated on their debut album 'Talking Heads '77', and its relentless, menacing single 'Psycho Killer', which became a punk anthem in the UK, although it had actually been one of the first songs Byrne, Frantz and Weymouth had written back in their early 70s Providence days. Both LP and single peaked at just below No.90 in the US charts early in 1978, which was almost the first commercial showing by any new wave act. In the UK, after two tours by the band (in mid-1977 with The Ramones, and in January 1978 as headliners on a trans-Europe trek), the album made No.60.

The Brian Eno-produced second album, 'More Songs About Buildings And Food', released in the summer of 1978, was a Top 30 success on both sides of the Atlantic. Despite effectively capturing the still-sharp quirkiness of their stage act, this album also began to highlight soul and world rhythm influences, as well as rapidly maturing songwriting skills, and from here on Talking Heads and punk effectively cut any remaining umbilical cord. The band maintained a cutting creative edge throughout their very successful next decade together, but they clearly grew (or wised) up more quickly than many of their contemporaries.

Recommended CD listening: 'Popular Favorites 1976-1992: Sand In The Vaseline' (Sire/Warner Bros. 9 26760-2)

THE TEARDROP EXPLODES

The Teardrop Explodes, a name lifted from, of all places, a caption in a Marvel superhero comic, were one of the most successful bands to come out of the thriving Liverpool punk/new wave scene of the late 1970s. They formed in October 1978, with an original line-up of Julian Cope (vocals and bass), Mick Finkler (guitar), Paul Simpson (keyboards) and Gary Dwyer (drums). Cope had previously rehearsed in 'almost' bands The Crucial Three, The Nova Mob and A Shallow Madness (the latter with Finkler and Simpson), alongside other local wannabees like Ian McCulloch, Pete Wylie and Budgie, but it was with The Teardrops that he finally had an outfit which actually got off the ground. They played their first live gig with McCulloch's equally new Echo & The Bunnymen at Eric's club in the November, and soon after that cut an EP, 'Sleeping Gas', for the local indie label Zoo Records.

In mid-1979, David Balfe, who had been co-managing the band with Zoo's Bill Drummond, took over on keyboards when Simpson departed for college. They toured widely across the UK, and had two more singles with Zoo, 'Bouncing Babies' and 'Treason (It's Just A Story)', which sold well enough, before being signed by Phonogram in the Summer of 1980 – though minus Finkler, who also quit for academia; his guitar replacement was Alan Gill, from Dalek I Love You.

The Phonogram deal quickly brought with it a first chart entry, as the next single 'When I Dream' scored at a moderate No.47 in the Autumn, swiftly followed by the band's debut album 'Kilimanjaro', which reached No.24 and was to have a 35-week run in the Top 75. The punchy, brass driven single 'Reward' finally bestowed a major commercial profile when it hit No.6 in February 1981, and put the band on *Top Of The Pops*. 'Treason' was resurrected as its follow-up, and made No.18.

After another hit single with 'Passionate Friend' (No.25), Gill left the band in Autumn 1981, initiating a period of personnel chopping and changing. Guitarist Troy Tate and bassist Ron Francois joined for the next album 'Wilder' (which reached No.29 at the end of the year), but both departed again the following July, while Balfe left and rejoined again in the interim. By the end of 1982, however, after extensive overseas touring and the band pared down to the trio of Cope, Dwyer and Balfe; individual ambitions and declining singles chart positions led to a feeling that The Teardrops had probably run their course, and in November they split, just four years to the day after that debut gig at Eric's. Cope would quickly start a solo career, which he would pursue into the 90s in fits and starts and with varying commercial success, while Balfe would move back to the non-performing side of the music industry, forming first a new management set-up and, eventually, the successful Food label. In 1990, an LP collection of previously unissued outtakes and other rarities, given the tongue-in-cheek title 'Everybody Wants To Shag The Teardrop Explodes', would – albeit briefly – resurrect the former band's name.

Recommended CD listening: 'Kilimanjaro' (Mercury 836897-2)

PUNK!

TELEVISION

Formed in New York at the tail-end of 1973, Television were seminal to the mid-70s punk scene in the Big Apple, yet they failed to find any proper commercial success in the US, and didn't last long enough to cash in on the commercial breakthrough of new wave music in America at the tail-end of the decade. During the initial UK punk explosion, however, they were revered as Yanks with the right sort of sound and attitude, and scored the British chart successes to underline this.

The band was formed by vocalist-guitarists Tom Verlaine (formerly Miller) and Richard Lloyd, who met in November 1973 at a New York club audition night. Verlaine had attempted to make a success of a band (The Neon Boys) two years previously, with his former schoolmates from Wilmington, Delaware, Richard Hell (nee Myers – bass) and Billy Ficca (drums). These two were re-recruited to make up what, in December, became Television. After two months of rehearsal, the quartet played their debut gig at the Townhouse Theatre on March 2, 1974, and for the next year became a fixture on the Manhattan club scene – notably at CBGB's, where they gained a weekly residency which started to attract similarly-minded new bands like The Ramones and Blondie to the venue.

In April 1975, Hell left after musical disagreements with Verlaine, to almost immediately resurface in The Heartbreakers. Television replaced him with Fred Smith, who had played in the original Blondie line-up, and the band finally made their recording debut with the single 'Little Johnny Jewel', forming their own independent Ork label to release it. A year later, however, a 'proper' deal finally came from Elektra Records, resulting, in February 1977, in the album 'Marquee Moon'. The band couldn't get arrested with this in America, but it had rave reviews in Britain and charted (No.28), as did the title track – all 20 minutes of it – on an extraordinary 12-inch single which climbed to No.30. On the back of these successes, they toured briefly in the UK with Blondie during May, and scored another Top 30 single with 'Prove It' (No.25) in August.

Early the following year, with a second album, 'Adventure', under their belts, the band returned to Britain for another short tour (having only played three US concerts in the previous 12 months), and got themselves two more UK hits, as in April the album soared to No.7 and the extracted single 'Foxhole' hit No.36. They must have returned to the US wondering exactly what they had to do to gain similar recognition at home, but in the event decided that it simply wasn't worth it: after playing six sell-out gigs at New York's Bottom Line Club late in August 1978, Television broke up. Verlaine got settled into a quite prolific solo career which was to take him through the 80s with critical plaudits but still little in the way of commercial success, while Lloyd also recorded solo. The second Television line-up was eventually to reunite in 1991, and they played a well-received set at the 1992 Glastonbury Fayre – in Britain, naturally.

Recommended CD listening: 'Marquee Moon' (Elektra 960616-2)

THOSE NAUGHTY LUMPS

Formed in Liverpool in the summer of 1977, the oddly-named Those Naughty Lumps originally comprised P.M. Hart, Tony Mitchell, Martin Armadillo, Peter 'Kid' Younger, and Kevin Wilkinson. They gained an early residency at the Havana Club, but stayed unrecorded until February 1979, when the band-penned 'Iggy Pop's Jacket' became one of the first singles on Bill Drummond's new Liverpool-based indie label, Zoo Records. This sold quite well on the indie market nationally, though was overshadowed by its companion release, The Teardrop Explodes' 'Sleeping Gas', and it was a long wait before the follow-up – a four-track EP on another Liverpool Indie, Open Eye Records, in mid-1980. By now there had been several personnel changes, with only Hart and Wilkinson remaining from the original line-up, and the band was not to last much longer beyond this point. Younger came back into the picture for a while in Wah! Heat, but otherwise The Lumps seemed content to ride into history.

THE TUBES

Although they were never strictly a punk band as such, The Tubes' anarchic and often controversial mixture of driving rock, flashy theatre, barbed satire and touches of pure outrage found them well in tune with punk audiences in the latter half of the 70s. The band, a large aggregation of musicians and female singer/dancers which could muster upwards of a dozen on stage, were led by a core of founder members Fee Waybill (vocals), Bill Spooner (guitar), Vince Welnick (keyboards) and Rick Anderson (bass). Signed to A&M in 1975, they made their major UK impact two years later, when the single 'White Punks On Dope', from their Al Kooper produced debut album 'The Tubes', hit the Top 30 at the height of the first commercial punk explosion. A lot of the punk audience presumably bought the record on face value, cherishing its outrage content – although, like 90% of The Tubes' output, it was actually digging frenetic fun at then-trendy nihilistic behaviour. The Tubes liked to buck the establishment all right, but hardly in the same way as The Sex Pistols.

The band had a second UK Top 40 hit in 1979 with 'Prime Time', while their A&M albums 'What Do You Want From Live' (a live album of the anarchic stage show) and 'Remote Control' also made the British charts in 1978 and '79. In the 80s, after a chalk-and-cheese pairing opposite Olivia Newton-John in the film *Xanadu*, they moved to Capitol Records, and had an American Top 10 hit in 1983 with the highly commercial but decidedly non-punk 'She's A Beauty'.

Recommended CD listening: 'The Best Of The Tubes' (Capitol 798359-2)

Television

UV

PUNK!

UK SUBS

Their name a shortened form of United Kingdom Subversives, The UK Subs were formed in London in 1977 (originally as The Marauders) by veteran rock and R&B vocalist and harmonica player Charlie Harper, a veteran of many years' dues-paying in assorted pub and club bands. Attracted by the random energy of punk, and unfazed by the fact that he was a decade older than most of the teenage musicians playing it around the Capital, Harper recruited Nick Garratt (guitar), Paul Slack (bass) and Peter Davies (drums). The Subs' first vinyl appearance was two live tracks on the 'Farewell To The Roxy' compilation album in April 1978, followed five months later by the Harper-penned single 'C.I.D.' on Indie City Records. In the spring of 1979, after building a reputation for rabble-rousing live shows, the band signed a recording deal with the GEM label, and their single 'Stranglehold' made No.26 in the chart – the start of a consistent two-year run of Top 40 singles, of which both 'Tomorrow's Girls' in September 1979 and 'Warhead' in March 1980 reached the Top 30, while the most offbeat was an EP led by a frantic punk-style reworking of the Zombies' 'She's Not There'!

The band also proved themselves to be able LP sellers. Their debut album 'Another Kind Of Blues' (which had blue sleeve, label and vinyl, but no discernible musical blues) made No.21 in October 1979, while the next year they hit No.18 with the follow-up 'Brand New Age', and an incredible No.8 with 'Crash Course', a live record of their kamikaze stage act, in which you can hear the audience growing ever more rowdy as the band breaks down into more and more chaos.

The last big-selling UK Subs album was 'Diminished Responsibility', which hit No.18 in March 1981, and spawned their last chart single 'Keep On Runnin' (Till You Burn)'. After this, they began to have major opposition coming from the burgeoning Oi! movement, with which The Subs were far too frivolous a band ever to identify. The curse of the ever-changing line-up also began to affect them, with Harper eventually being the only fixture in a constantly-shifting personnel which began, in the mid-80s, to embrace rowdy heavy metal elements alongside the raucous punk. Harper has never stopped performing, and never let The Subs name die (also continuing to record regularly – there was an average album a year throughout the 80s and early 90s), but the band now effectively represents a punk oldies revival show, and has not managed to achieve any commercial bite for more than a decade.

Recommended CD listening: 'Another Kind Of Blues' (Trance/Line TCCD 9005320)

Undertones

THE UNDERTONES

Northern Ireland's premier punk band formed in Londonderry at the latter end on 1975. The initial prime movers were O'Neill brothers John (guitar) and Damian (guitar), joined by Michael Bradley (bass) and Billy Doherty (drums). Former school classmate Feargal Sharkey, a winning veteran of youth talent contests, was then recruited as vocalist. After a couple of uneventful years on the Derry gigging circuit, The Undertones recorded the EP 'Teenage Kicks' in June 1978 for Terri Hooley's Belfast-based indie label Good Vibrations, after receiving rejections from Radar, Stiff and Chiswick. The title song immediately found favour with Radio 1's John Peel, who called it one of the finest singles he had ever heard, and his championing of it on the air also alerted the US-based Sire label, which despatched an emissary to Belfast to buy up Good Vibrations' rights and offer the band a deal. Reissued nationally in October 1978, 'Teenage Kicks' sprinted to

No.31 in the UK chart, and began a near two-year run of seven hit singles for the band on Sire, including a Top 20 entry (No.16) with the urgent 'Jimmy Jimmy' in May 1979, and two even bigger successes the following year with the melodic and pop-sensitive 'My Perfect Cousin' (No.9) and 'Wednesday Week' (No.11). Two Sire albums, 'The Undertones' in June 1979 and the Netherlands-recorded 'Hypnotised' in May 1980, climbed to Nos 13 and 6 respectively, the debut album racking up an impressive 21-week residency in the chart.

Despite a major US tour during 1979 with The Clash, and headlining US and European tours the following year, Sire surprisingly failed to break The Undertones' perkily poppy punk style to significant commercial success

outside the British Isles, and in October 1980, with their two-year deal expired, the band launched their own Ardeck label through EMI. A new album, 'Positive Touch', made No.17 the following May, and at the same time spun off 'It's Going To Happen!', the band's swansong Top 20 single. The follow-up 'Julie Ocean', however, despite widespread airplay, proved disappointing, and halted one place short of the Top 40.

Almost two years passed before 'The Sin Of Pride', The Undertones' final album of new material, which only made No.43. Despite continuing live popularity, internal frustration over the band's restricted scope for development was pressuring them to split, which they did in June 1983. The disbandment was marked by a reissue of 'Teenage Kicks', which went

on to enjoy a brief second run in the charts. The retrospective album 'All Wrapped Up' also charted at the end of the year, while Sharkey briefly teamed up with Vince Clarke (ex-Yazoo) as The Assembly, and scored a No.4 hit with 'Never, Never'. He would go on to a highly successful solo career (including a No.1 hit with 'A Good Heart') through the second half of the 80s, before eventually eschewing performance in favour of a major record company A&R job. The rest of the ex-Undertones did not manage quite the same high profile, but the O'Neill brothers also had a healthy series of chart successes with That Petrol Emotion.

Recommended CD listening: 'Cher O'Bowlies (Pick Of The Undertones)' (EMI/Fame CDFA 3226)

PUNK!

THE VAPORS

From Guildford, Surrey, The Vapors were a Mod-influenced punk band who, shortly after their formation in April 1979, were to become proteges of The Jam, supporting the latter on their 'Setting Sons' UK tour, and being jointly managed by Jam bassist Bruce Foxton and Paul Weller's father John. The band comprised Dave Fenton (vocals and guitar), Edward Bazalgette (guitar), Steve Smith (bass) and Howard Smith (drums), all of whom had played in earlier bands of little significance.

Signed by United Artists in September 1979, they debuted a month later with the unsuccessful single 'Prisoners', but turned their fortunes around the following spring when the manically catchy 'Turning Japanese' shot to No.3. Later suggestions that the song was concerned with changing sexual identity didn't occur to anybody at the time, and the song received blanket UK airplay. It also achieved something The Jam never managed by cracking the American chart, where it peaked at a respectable No.36. The album 'New Clear Days' followed, packed with similarly succinct pop-punk anthems, though it was slightly more muted in chart terms, peaking at No.44 – which curiously was also the position reached by both the band's follow-up singles, 'News At Ten' and (a year later, in mid-1981) 'Jimmy Jones'. The latter came from the second Vapors album 'Magnets', which hardly rated a note from the critics, and sank without trace. After this, with Jam comparisons (long outgrown) still hanging around their necks albatross-fashion, the band found it impossible to make further headway, and had broken up by the end of the year.

THE VELVET UNDERGROUND

Although the key work of The Velvet Underground (Lou Reed, John Cale, Stirling Morison and Maureen Tucker) pre-dated the mid-70s punk explosion by almost a full decade, it is difficult to overstate the effect of this band's *in absentia* influence on the later genre. Along with The New York Dolls, Iggy & The Stooges and The MC5, The Velvets were one of the prime sources upon which the first punk generation leaned, and from whose stance it freely pilfered. Punk identified with the uncompromising attitudes to audience and convention which these bands had demonstrated, and it eagerly echoed their ready conversion of conflict and inner torment into angry, aggressive musical expression. Reed & Co., in particular, also bequeathed the alienating, intimidatory element which much of their music projected. This uneasy sense of menace beneath the surface, capable of leaving the listener at odds with his own emotional reaction, was the essence of what made The Velvet Underground unique, but during the late 1960s, this tended to restrict their commercial potential to cult acceptance by the musically adventuresome. By the mid-70s, the punk movement was interested in overt musical alienation and intimidation: it was an essential element of their basic message, which was up yours! to the musical and

social establishment status quo of the day.

Not a lot of The Velvets' actual musical style was transposed directly into punk in the first instance, although it was notable that John Cale, as a producer, was an early and quite prolific player in the punk recording field, with sometimes sublime and perhaps occasionally ridiculous results. It was more an identification with the spirit of a band which swam doggedly against the commercial tide of its time, which touched several kinds of darkness and gave them breathtaking expression, and perhaps most of all, looked cool and made a bloody loud racket, which gave punk its hard to deny debt to The Velvet Underground.

Recommended CD listening: 'Velvet Underground And Nico' (Polydor 823290-2) and 'Best Of The Velvet Underground' (Polydor Verve 841164-2)

THE VIBRATORS

Formed in London in February 1976, and comprising Knox (Ian Carnochan – vocals), John Ellis (guitar), Pat Collier (bass) and Eddie (John Edwards – drums), The Vibrators were essentially an R&B-orientated pub band, first coming to punk notice when they played (curiously, with session guitarist Chris Spedding) at the 100 Club Punk Festival in September that year. Their first single, released shortly after and recorded with Spedding (and issued by RAK, which had him contracted) was the blatant cash-in 'Pogo Dancing', but by April 1977 the band signed (without Spedding) to CBS and recorded the album 'Pure Mania', which was mostly pure high-octane punk rock, and made No.49 in the chart. Gary Tibbs came in at the point on bass to replace Collier, and the band entered their highest-profile stage, touring widely around the UK, across Europe (spending some months based in Berlin) and as far as Canada. A hit single (reaching No.35) came in March 1978 with 'Automatic Lover', but hot on its heels, and immediately prior to the release of the second album 'V2' (a No.32 hit), Ellis left for a solo recording career (and to play with Peter Gabriel), and a new line-up including David Birch on guitar and Don Snow on keyboards, recorded the band's second and last minor hit single 'Judy Says (Knock You In The Head)'. By now, Knox felt they were drifting away from the punk musical fashion, and in danger of being in a musical limbo. They split in the summer, Knox and Eddie did a few more appearances (with more new musicians) in the early Autumn, and they finally bowed out at London's Marquee club in October 1978. Almost a year later, drummer Eddie announced a re-formed aggregation under The Vibrators name, but his new band, with former players from Eater and The Electric Chairs on board, had only the most tenuous musical connections with its predecessor, and failed to attract much notice.

Recommended CD listening: 'The Power Of Money (The Best Of The Vibrators)' (Anagram CDGRAM 52)

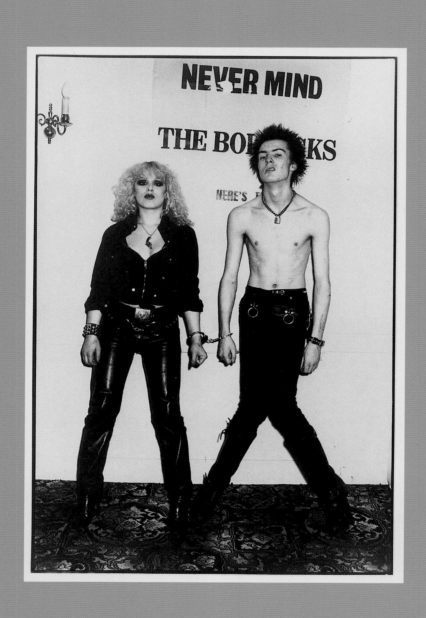

VICE SQUAD

Vice Squad came together in Bristol during 1979, combining elements from two local teenage gigging bands, TV Brakes and The Contingent. The four-piece comprised Beki Bondage (whose mother knew her as Rebecca Bond) on vocals, with Dave Bateman (guitar), Mark Hambly (bass) and Shane Baldwin (drums). Together they combined a tough, spiky punk image while playing music which veered between straight-ahead aggressive rock and tuneful power-pop, and soon discovered that they had a potent image focus on Bondage, who, while never overtly outrageous by the standards of Riot Girl bands of later years, allowed the rock media to trumpet her as punk's leading sex symbol. She did pose topless on one occasion for the front cover of *Sounds*, but (the cause of grumbling readers' letters) only with her back to the camera.

Unable to attract a record deal during their early months of gigging, the band formed their own Riot City label, which issued their debut single 'Last Rockers' in December 1980. This was followed by the 'Resurrection' EP, after which both band and label were signed by the EMI Zonophone division, and the album 'No Cause For Concern' was released, to a muted critical reception but decent enough sales – it reached No.32 in the UK album chart. Only seven months later, a second album, 'Stand Strong, Stand Proud', was in the shops (and the chart, at No.47). However, apart from a brief chart touch (a week at 68) by 'Out Of Reach' between the two albums, Vice Squad's Zonophone singles did not build their commercial profile as EMI planned, and relations within the band and with the record company began to sour. This resulted in Bondage's departure during 1983, to record the single 'Crime And Passion' for EMI with new musicians, as Ligotage. By this time, the music press's tabloid-like infatuation with her as a punk sex symbol had abated, and Ligotage went rapidly down the road to nowhere. Vice Squad recruited new girl vocalist Lia and released a third album, 'Shot Away', but it meant little sales-wise and the band rapidly faded from view thereafter.

Recommended CD listening: 2 tracks on 'Riot City: The Punk Singles Collection' (Anagram CDPUNK 15)

THE VORTEX

Aside from the Roxy in Covent Garden, the Vortex Club at 201, Wardour Street was arguably the highest-profile punk venue in London's West End during the late 1970s. Arriving some seven months after the Roxy came on the scene, the Vortex had a high-profile opening featuring Siouxsie & The Banshees, Sham 69, The Slits and Adam & The Ants, on July 11, 1977. Spirits ran sufficiently high at the venue that night for the police to check out a breach of the peace, and Sham's Jimmy Pursey was seized upon as the perpetrator of said breach. He was later fined £30, which probably depleted his band's fee for the gig quite considerably.

A live various artists compilation album, 'Live At The Vortex, Vol.1', was taped at the venue and released on NEMS Records in December 1977. The somewhat mixed bag of (then unsigned) acts it captured for punk posterity included The Art Attacks, The Maniax, Mean Street, Neo, The Suspects, Bernie Torme and The Wasps.

Vivienne Westwood

Vivienne Westwood was Malcolm McLaren's partner in most of his early business ventures in the mid-1970s, notably the Kings Road shops where the genesis of The Sex Pistols took place. The first incarnation of their shop at 430 Kings Road, opened in 1971, was Let It Rock, dedicated to The Teddy Boy style and 50s culture in general, and selling long drape jackets, brocade waistcoats, and clingy V-neck t-shirts for the pony-tailed rocker girl. In the Spring of 1973, sensing that 50s retro-chic was past its prime, Westwood and McLaren remodelled the shop as Too Fast To Live, Too Young To Die, which expanded its ethos to include 60s mod styles and American 50s teen clothing. (It was in this period of the business that future Pistol Glen Matlock first got a Saturday sales job, and where he got to know Steve Jones and Paul Cook, who came in to occasionally buy clothes and more generally hang around).

By the middle of 1974, Westwood and McLaren were thinking along different lines again. The shop was briefly closed, to reopen as Sex (they called themselves 'Specialists in rubberware, glamourwear and stagewear'), one of the world's first deliberately seditious clothes stores. Sex offered rubber t-shirts, skirts and suits, leather and vinyl tops, and ripped t-shirts adorned with political and sexual slogans. Elements of the archetypal punk wardrobe were created by Westwood right here, although the aim at the time was to emphasise sexual fantasy for the young. 'Wearing these clothes will affect your social life', said the shop's publicity blurb. 'Ordinary fashion is just concerned with beauty factors to the exclusion of social ones'. McLaren described Westwood's creations for Sex as 'an affront to the established way of doing things', and this affront was indeed taken seriously by the establishment when, in August 1975, both he and Westwood were prosecuted for an 'indecent exhibition' in one of the shop's displays.

Westwood moved into rock'n'roll management along with McLaren as soon as the pair became involved with The Sex Pistols. As well as her advice and ideas being behind much of the band's visual image, and what became standard punk band 'uniform', she was not above immersing herself in The Pistols' celebrated anti-social lifestyle. A notable example was at a gig in April 1976 at London's Nashville Rooms, during which Westwood allegedly picked on a member of the audience and a scuffle ensued – into which three of The Pistols, abandoning the stage, also dived. Photos taken on the spot show Westwood in the thick of it, with a space-out Sid Vicious looking on like the bystander from hell. The Pistols were banned from the Nashville thereafter - the start of an honourable tradition! In later post-Pistols days, Westwood disentangled herself from the punk rock world, but not from her always unconventional and uncompromising ideas on fashion, and she eventually made the mainstream British fashion world as its resident *enfant terrible*. Yesterday she put Johnny Rotten in rips, zips and safety pins; today she puts Naiomi Campbell in heels so stratospheric that she supermodel overbalances on the catwalk and greets the canvas. With both scenarios, public awareness of Westwood's work soars. *Plus ca change.*

THE WALL

The Wall were formed in Sunderland at the end of 1977, and originally comprised Ian Lowery (vocals), Nick Ward (guitar), Andy Griffiths (bass) and Rabfae Beith (drums). In 1979, like many other punk bands of the era, they got their start on record via a deal with Small Wonder – though, unlike most others, their tenure with the label stretched beyond the usual one-off to two singles: 'New Way' midway through the year was followed a few months later by 'Kiss The Mirror', which was still selling early in 1980 – it stood at No.26 in the first UK indie chart in February. By this time, Lowery had left the band (he would eventually re-emerge in the folk devils), and the new vocalist was Kelly, formerly with Ruefrex.

1980 saw the first Wall album, 'Personal Troubles And Public Issues' (a fair description of the contents), following a label switch to Fresh Records. It also saw further movement in the ranks, first as new guitarist Heed joined, temporarily upping the line-up to a quintet, and then as both Kelly and Ward departed. Opting to continue as a trio, the band were signed by Polydor in 1981, but apart from delivering a couple of modestly successful singles and another album, the major label liaison was not a happy one, marred as it was by conflict over musical direction and the way Polydor wanted the band marketed. The subsequent parting was inevitable, but seemed to take the steam out of the band (who were additionally feeling the effect of the proliferation of Oi! bands – a scene with which they could not identify), and they made just one more small label resurgence, cutting a cranked-up version of the Beatles' 'Day Tripper' for No Future (ironically, an Oi!-orientated label) before sinking from view.

WIRE

Wire, one of the more intellectually-regarded new bands to spring into prominence during the punk era, formed in the spring of 1976, when the members were at art college. The original line-up was a five-piece, with Bruce Gilbert (vocals & guitar), Colin Newman (vocals & guitar), George Gill (guitar), Graham Lewis (bass & vocals), and ex-Art Attacks member Rob Gotobed (drums). Gill left in January 1977, prior to the band's first recording as part of EMI/Harvest's live punk collection 'The Roxy, London WC2'. The remaining quartet were then signed to a full deal by Harvest and teamed with producer Mike Thorne, who helped to give them a hard, spare studio sound quite unlike that of any of their contemporaries, allied to lyrics which showed them as angry young men with ideas, as opposed to the lash-out-at-all approach of more nihilistic (and less musically sound) fellow travellers. The debut album 'Pink Flag', issued in the Autumn of 1978, was a 21-track feast of short sharp shocks, and appealed to record buyers sufficiently to rise to No.48. The second set, 'Chairs Missing', was also found missing from the charts, possibly the result of Wire's refusal to aim at a more commercial, less committed sound in the way many other punk-originated bands were by early 1979. However, '154', following later that year, sold well again, peaking at No.39. Effectively, though, this wound up Wire in its original form, because the band, somewhat like The Beatles a decade earlier, was proving unable to contain the variant ideas and ambitions of its members – or, more specifically, Newman on one hand, and Lewis and Gilbert on the other. After a final live gig at the

Electric Ballroom in London in 1980, (captured on the album 'Document And Eyewitness'), they split: Newman began to record as a soloist, and Lewis and Gilbert as a duo which would develop into Dome. (Gotobed, meanwhile, went into session work and then joined Fad Gadget). The New Wave experimentation of these post-Wire adventures effectively removed them for good from the punk umbrella. Interestingly, though, they didn't, in the long run, remove Wire permanently from the scene – the band would eventually re-form as techno-influenced rockers in 1987. Possibly Wire's best-remembered track, by the way, was their single 'Map Ref. 41 degrees N, 93 degrees W' – which, according to those who had taken the trouble to follow it up in an atlas, was Des Moines, Iowa. Nobody quite seems to know why, but that was the inscrutability of Wire for you.

Recommended CD listening: 'On Returning' (Harvest CDP 792535-2)

Wreckless Eric

WRECKLESS ERIC

Real name Eric Goulden, Wreckless emerged from the tail-end of pub-rock in time to be one of the early signees to Stiff Records, and, like his compatriots Elvis Costello and Nick Lowe, to be regarded as a punk by association. Eric was fresh and original, and had a ramshackle demeanour that Sid Vicious might have admired, but the nihilism and anti-musicianship of The Pistols and their ilk were not strictly his forte: instead, he was an inventive songwriter, and produced tuneful 'real' numbers like 'Reconnaez Cherie', 'Hit And Miss Judy' and 'Whole Wide World', all of which consistently and curiously failed to chart, despite a high profile through 1977/78, nurtured by Stiff's effective grassroots PR and a widely applauded live act which relished in the typical off-kilter energy of the time, and simply allowed Goulden to be Wreckless. He was part of the legendary Stiffs Live UK tour-by-train in October 1977, alongside label-mates, Costello, Lowe, Larry Wallis and Ian Dury & The Blockheads, and is heard in his prime on the 'Live Stiffs Live' compilation album which the trek produced.

When UK success passed him by, Eric turned to Europe, in particular France, where his style had built him an early and faithful audience. He continues to play, on both sides of the Channel, to the present day, and made some quirky and applauded – though usually difficult to find – indie label recordings under the *nom-du-disque* of the Len Bright Combo during the latter years of the 1980s.

Recommended CD listening: 'Wreckless Eric '(Repertoire 4217 WY)

PUNK!

X-Ray Specs with Lora Logic on sax and Poly Styrene on vocals

X

One of the very first bands to make their mark on the Los Angeles late-70s punk scene, X were formed in 1977, taking their minimalist name from that of female lead vocalist Exene (real name Christine Cervenka, originally from Chicago). The other original members were Billy Zoom (guitar), John Doe (bass and vocals, real name Nommensen) and Mick Basher (drums) – although by the time the quartet made their vinyl debut in April 1978, with the single 'Adult Books'/'We're Desperate' for the indie Dangerhouse label, the latter had been replaced behind the drumkit by Don J. Bonebrake, previously with The Eyes.

Their powerhouse blend of punk nihilism with heavy metal and a touch of rockabilly (Zoom had once backed Gene Vincent) built the band a solid gigging reputation in L.A. Most local labels, however, found them hard to come to terms with, and it was not until mid-1980 that a deal with Slash Records saw them featured on the 'Decline Of Western Civilisation' compilation and their own debut album 'Los Angeles', which was produced by former Doors member Ray Manzarek.

A second Slash album, 'Wild Gift', in mid-1981, actually saw the band into the US charts (a modest No.165), and aroused the interest of the Elektra label, which signed them early in 1982. Major label promotion helped the next three albums into the US top 100 – 'Under The Big Black Sun' (1982) reached 76, 'More Fun In The New World' (1983) 86, and 'Ain't Love Grand' (1985) 89. At this point, Zoom left, and was replaced by former Blasters guitarist Dave Alvin, with whom Exene and Doe had already been playing in a country sideline band named the Knitters.

For 1987's 'See How You Are' album, the band expanded to a quintet with the addition of former Lone Justice guitarist Tony Gilkyson, but neither this nor the follow-up double live LP 'Live At The Whiskey A-Go-Go On The Fabulous Sunset Strip' quite equalled the commercial success of the previous albums, or their power: the live set displayed a band demonstrably less radical or barnstorming than its original late-70s incarnation. Presumably, X thought so themselves – they split within months of the album's release, with Doe striking out as a solo artist.

X-RAY SPEX

With a name and image that seemed to many to encapsulate the whole lighter side of the UK punk movement (ie the energy and the peacock expressionism, rather than the anger and nihilism), the Spex were one of the many spontaneously-combining teenage combos who became known to most record buyers through appearing on the Harvest label's 1977 live album 'The Roxy, London WC2', before cutting a one-off for Virgin – 'Oh Bondage, Up Yours' – which in turn became one of the archetypal punk era catch phrases, even though the single never actually made any of the charts.

The band was built around vocalist and songwriter Polly Styrene (whose parents knew her better as Marion Elliot. Not the most obviously glamorous of teenagers (she was decidedly un-willowy and wore a brace on her teeth), Polly turned her appearance consciously into a punk image, enhancing it with colourful clothes whose individualism marked her out even at the height of punk fashion. The rest of the original group were Lora Logic on saxophone, Jak Stafford on guitar, Paul Dean on bass, and B.P. Hurding on drums. By the time they were signed to a full recording deal by EMI's International division, Lora had departed to do her own thing in Essential Logic, and Glyn Johns came in on sax. The EMI releases came at the time of punk's biggest commercial breakthrough, and four anthemic, energetic X-Ray Spex singles – 'The Day The World Turned Day-Glo', 'Identity', 'Germ-Free Adolescence' and 'Highly Inflammable' – all made the UK charts within a period of 12 months, as did their excellent 'Germ-Free Adolescence' album, which in later years would be regarded as a classic, a punk collector's item of great desirability.

The band did not, however, outlast the 1970s – not because of any decline in their appeal or record sales, but simply because Styrene had had enough of the rock business roundabout and its demands upon her life. When she voiced her decision to quit, the band was effectively over, so pivotal was her role within it.

Post-Spex, Polly demonstrated the strength of her convictions by joining the Hare Krishna movement, (as did her former band-mate Lora Logic). Her occasional solo musical forays in later years have been both low-key and very few and far between.

Recommended CD listening: 'Germ-Free Adolescence'(Virgin CDVM 9001)

XTC

Formed in Swindon in 1977, and known as Star Park and The Helium Kids before they hit on the idea of expressing the word 'Ecstasy' as XTC, this was one of the many bands initially tarred with the punk brush more because of the time of their arrival on the scene and the kind of audience and rock press attention they attracted, than because of any particularly strong punk edge to their style. In fact, XTC were the thoughful, quirky face of New Wave some two years before their time, and this may have had some bearing on their suprisingly ambivilant relationship with commercial success (as many puzzlingly poor-selling albums as chartmakers), despite a subsqunt career spanning the 80s.

The band pivoted around vocalist/guitarist/songwriter Andy Partridge, whose slightly offbeat and eccentric take on life in general has always been the fuel of XTC's best material. The rest of the original 1977 line-up were ex-King Crimson player Barry Andrews (keyboards), Colin Moulding (bass) and Terry Chambers (drums). Playing their initial London dates in the summer, they were then signed to Virgin, debuting on record with the '3D-EP', which, ususually, was available only on 12-inch. This, and the lack of an identifiable A-side to hook radio programmers, probably contributed to its lack of chart progress. They took a while to make any impression with singles, unlike most punky contemporaries, who found it easy to shift the two-minute 7-inchers and far harder to convince buyer to part with the price of a half-hour album. XTC, by contast, shone in the longer format, and both their 1978 albums, the quickly-recorded 'White Music' and the more sophisticated 'Go 2', made the UK album charts.

Andrews left the band (eventually to join Shriekback) at the beginning of 1979, and was replaced on keyboards by Dave Gregory, who arrived in time to share in XTC's period of greatest commercial success. It was at this time that they made the Top 30 with the singles 'Making Plans For Nigel' and 'Generals And Majors', toured in the US and the Pacific Rim, placed a song alongside contributions of other UK punks and new-wavers on the soundtrack of the movie *Times Square*, and continued to record chartmaking albums in the shapes of 'Drums And Wires' and 'Black Sea' (which also took them into the American charts).

By 1981, punk had dissipated and many of its leading light acts had either split or widened their musical horizons. Having been touched only circumstantially by the movement, Partridge (who began a parallel solo recording career too, and wasn't afraid to wear his glasses any more) and XTC merely continued in their individual groove, and settled down as elders statesmen of New Wave in the by-now burgeoning world of the New Romantics. By *that* particular standard, of course, with their sharp, spiky observations and lack of pretention, XTC were very punk indeed.

Recommended CD listening: 'The Compact XTC' (Virgin CDV 2251)

 XTC

THE YACHTS

Formed in Liverpool in April 1977, the Yachts (who originally called Albert Dock & The Codfish Warriors!) consisted of five art students: J.J. Campbell (vocals), Henry Priestman (vocals & keyboards), Martin J. Watson (guitar), Martin Dempsey (bass) and Bob Bellis (drums). Their big break came after six months of local gigging, when a support slot with Elvis Costello at Liverpool's punk music hub Eric's led to them being noticed by his label, Stiff, with subsequent release of the single 'Suffice To Say'. (At the same time, they also moonlighted, as the 'Chuddy Nuddies' on 'Do The Chud', one side of a single shared with Big In Japan on Eric's own label).

The Stiff deal got the band some London dates, but was short-lived, as the band shifted at the end of 1977 to Jake Riviera's new Radar label, alongside Costello and Nick Lowe. At the same time, they became a four piece, when Campbell left and Priestman took over the frontman/vocalist role. Radar issued seven, mostly critically-rated, singles over the next two years, including 'Look Back In Love (Not In Anger)', 'Yachting Types' and a revival of R. Dean Taylor's 'There's A Ghost In My House', but none made the chart, and neither did the album 'Yachts', recorded in New York with producer Richard Gottehrer while they were playing US dates.

In January 1980, Dempsey left to join Pink Military, and Mick Shiner took over on bass, in time for the wryly-titled second album 'Yachts Without Radar', which was promoted by a European tour with the Who, but seemed to be commenting on both the band's frustrating lack of upward progress and the lachrymose state of their label. By the end of the year, Radar was indeed no more, and in 1981 they followed Riviera again (with another new bass player, Glyn Havard, formerly of the Edge) to his new Demon label, where 'A Fool Like You' became their swansong single not long before a final split. Priestman then joined It's Immaterial, but would eventually find major commercial success in 1987 with the Christians.

THE ZONES

The Glasgow-based Zones were an unusual example of a punk-orientated band which evolved from a pre-punk outfit with a successful past – namely Slik, who had topped the UK singles chart with 'Forever And Ever' in January 1976. The advent of punk had severely marginalised Slik's glam-pop style, and in 1977, in something of an identitiy crisis, they changed their name and updated their sound to cut the single 'Put You In The Picture' under the name of PVC 2 for the new Edinburgh indie label Zoom Records. The anonymity of the name change mitigated against the single getting any wide exposure, and within weeks of its release, lead singer and guitarist Midge Ure split to London to join ex-Pistol Glen Matlock's Rich Kids. Other members Billy McIsaac (keyboards), Russell Webb (bass) and Kenny Hyslop (drums) recruited vocalist/guitarist Willie Gardner (formerly with the Hot Valves), and they renamed themselves the Zones, releasing a Webb song, 'Stuck With You' on Zoom, though despite a couple of name-boosting support slots with The Clash, this didn't sell either. However, when the Zoom label and roster was sold to Arista, the bigger label put some weight behind the band, and they toured and recorded throughout 1978 and most of '79, even cutting an album – 'Under Influence' – in June 1979, despite the fact that none of their three self-penned singles released on Arista made the chart.

Eventually, in November 1979, The Zones tired of their non-breakthrough and split. Webb moved straight to the Skids, who had just suffered a desertion of personnel. Just over a year later, Hyslop joined him there, and six months after that, would play for a while with Simple Minds.

PUNK!

The publishers would like to thank all those who supplied photographic material for use in this book and apologize to any whose contribution may have been inadvertently omitted from these acknowledgements. We are particularly grateful to Robert Matthews, Barry Plummer, and the staff at LFI, Redferns and Retna for their help with this project.

Camera Press /Ray Hamilton 7, /R. Hamilton 38, 39, /Derek Ridgers 62 top centre, 62 centre right, 62 bottom right, /Derek Ridges 62 bottom centre

Cherry Red Records /1979 44 right

Chiswick Records 29 centre left

Clay Records 47

Demon Records Ltd/Stiff 41 background image Roger Eaton 150, 151

Deborah Feingold 5

John Frost Historical Newspapers 85 Ronald Grant Archive 71, 76 bottom

Hulton Deutsch Collection 115, 152 Hutchison Library 142 /143

Impact /Christopher Pillitz 64

Island 127 right

London Features International 148, /Santo Basone 8, 90, /Adrian Boot 94, /Paul Cox 46, 52, 54 top, 127 left, /Simon Fowler 29 bottom right, 34 bottom, 80, 96 97, /Jill Furmanowsky 29 centre right, /Jill Furnmanovsky 133, /Chris Gaerin 37, /Jill Furmanovsky 61, /Steve Rapport 29 bottom left, 36 Top, /Ann Summa 43

Magnum Photos /Burt Glinn 63 bottom left, /Peter Marlow 92 /93

PUNK!

New Musical Express 110, 132

Barry Plummer 10, 12, 13, 20 /21, 35, 45, 49, 53, 59, 60 left, 69 bottom, 69 top, 73, 77 top, 81, 83, 87 right, 88, 123 bottom, 124, 130, 131 top left, 135, 144 /145

Redferns /Richie Aaron 117, /Glenn A. Baker Archives 122, /Glen A. Baker Archives 156, /Glenn A Baker Archives 157 top left, /Ian Dickson 41 left, 108 /109, 111, 112, /Erica Echenberg 56, 98 /99, 99, 123 top, 147, 155, /Ebet Roberts 40, 42, 139, 141, /Gems 23, 67, 79, 128, /Chris Mills 102, /S. Morley 74, /RB 121, /David Redfern 19, /Steve Richards 114, /Ebet Roberts 17, 27 top, 27 bottom right, 27 centre left, 75, 89 top, 89 bottom, 154, /S&G 134, /John Tiberi 87 left, 152 Refill Records 44 left

Jamie Reid 7, 68, 84, 100, 158 /159

Retna /Adrian Boot 32 bottom, 103, /David Corio 54 bottom, /Kevin Davies 86, /Steve Double 62 top left, /Michel Goron 63, /Malcolm Heywood 34 top, /Joseph King 104, /Tony Mottram 9 bottom, /Michael Putland 48, /Patrick Quigly 26, /Paul Slattery 16 /17, 30, 32 top, 33, /Ray Stevenson 9 top, 18, 22 bottom, 25, 29 top, 41 right, 65, 78

Rex Features 125, /EAD 136 /137, /Nils Jorgensen 62 centre left, 62 top right, /Ray Stevenson 22 top

Riot City Records 149

Rough Trade 109, 129

SPZ/'by courtesy of Stiff Records' 82, 131 bottom, 131 top right Stiff Records 15, 131 top right below, 131 top right centre Virgin Records Ltd 156 inset

Zoom Records 157 top right

Thanks also to all those people who kindly lent us their records, record covers and other material, especially Zep Gerson and Richard Scott.